PRAISE FOR *WINNING IN Y〰〰〰*

"Dena's book hits home. She reflects on [elements of] unhealthy law firm cultures like micromanagement, misogyny, and misery and how to overcome them. This book is a must if you want to discover your real purpose, feel valued, have more confidence, and simply enjoy your career more. A profession in law should not be a disappointment. Learn how your life in law can be more rewarding, inspiring, and meaningful by reading this book and taking Dena's counsel to heart."

—Gina F. Rubel, Esq., founder and CEO,
Furia Rubel Communications, Inc.

"An exquisite book that reads like a novel, behaves like a self-help guide, and should be on every desk—not shelf—of lawyers, authors, and C-suite executives. Dena Lefkowitz deftly turns stumbling blocks into stepping stones that lead us into the clearing [to find] the careers and people we want to become and show us in her own words how our personalities either hinder or help [us] achieve our goals."

—Terry L. Mutchler, Esq., author and partner at
Obermayer Rebmann Maxwell & Hippel, LLP

"Dena captures universal truths applicable to any pursuit and makes the point—so important to attorneys—that it's not enough to make thunder and lightning. You've got to make rain. This book provides a taste of what it's like to have a coach in your corner, as I have [had] with Dena for many years, to help you in your journey."

—James J. Rohn, Esq., Co-Founder, Rohn Kurland, PC

"Now more than ever, lawyers seek to design a satisfying professional life that aligns with the intrinsic forces that drew them to law school, gives them agency over their work and time, and elevates meaning and purpose over status and achievement. Drawing from deeply personal experiences in 'learning the hard way,' Dena Lefkowitz lays out clear, actionable steps law students and lawyers can follow to feel better, experience deep and lasting professional pride and engagement, and serve clients with excellence."

—Jennifer Leonard, chief innovation officer and executive director, Future of the Profession Initiative, University of Pennsylvania Carey Law School

"In clear, direct, and surprisingly graceful prose, this book provides a set of guidelines intended to help lawyers maximize their career development. On the one hand, this kind of information is not available in law school or on the job; it is the product of experience and reflection by a highly seasoned practitioner who knows whereof she speaks. On the other hand, the insightful career advice laid out in this book is applicable to careers in any field, from medicine to engineering to song writing. It is a sensible and highly pertinent guide to modern career advancement."

—Dr. Robert Hogan, founder, Hogan Assessments

"Framed by honest personal experience and accented by Dena's compassionate work with her coaching clients, this work will be a valuable resource for lawyers who have gotten stuck and lost sight of their North Star. It's a manual for rediscovering what makes you tick and what work speaks to that."

—Rick Linsk, journalist and lawyer

AMERICAN**BAR**ASSOCIATION

ABA Publishing

Winning in Your Own Court

10 Laws for a Successful Career without Burning Out or Selling Out

Dena Lefkowitz

Cover design by Elmarie Jara/ABA Design

Printed in the United States of America.

26 25 24 23 22   5 4 3 2 1

Library of Congress Cataloging-in-Publication Data
Names: Lefkowitz, Dena, author.
Title: Winning in your own court : 10 laws for a successful career without burning out or selling out / Dena Lefkowitz.
Description: Chicago, Illinois : American Bar Association, [2022} | Summary: "As I've worked coaching lawyers over the last decade or so, I've seen that for the most part they are as unprepared to guide their own careers as I was when I graduated from law school in 1988. They, too, feel the tension between who they are deep down and who their workplaces are asking them to be. Helping those who practice law to resolve that tension and have the life and career they see for themselves is why I became a coach and why I wrote this book. From my own experience and from working with clients, I now have developed a framework like the one I used to so many years ago, but it's specific to a career in law. This set of ten laws-laws no one ever taught us in law school-has taken hundreds of my clients and their careers from default to design"--Provided by publisher.
Identifiers: LCCN 2022009786 | ISBN 9781639051304 (paperback) | ISBN 9781639051311 (ebook)
Classification: LCC KF297 .L45 2022 | DDC 340.023/73--dc23/eng/20220526
LC record available at https://lccn.loc.gov/2022009786

Discounts are available for books ordered in bulk. Special consideration is given to state bars, CLE programs, and other bar-related organizations. Inquire at Book Publishing, ABA Publishing, American Bar Association, 321 N. Clark Street, Chicago, Illinois 60654-7598.

www.shopABA.org

This book is dedicated to my wonderful husband, Rolando Corpus,
who always encourages me in my life and career
and who cheerfully read every draft. Thank you, honey.

Contents

Introduction: From the Back of the Room to the Supreme Court

When I was growing up in an Orthodox Jewish family, our synagogue (we called it *shul*, its Yiddish name) had a "men's section" and a "women's section." Services were held in a converted single home with a large first floor. The women's section was in the back, separated from the men's section by a room divider made of solid wood on the bottom and a thick lattice screen at the top. When seated during services, women and girls stared at the wood. When we rose, the lattice blocked a clear view of the bema and ark, where the Torah was housed, and we couldn't see anything more definite than the shadowy shapes of male congregants receiving the honor of being called to read from the Torah.

Men directed the entire service and were the only active participants. My father and brothers left for *shul* early to join their fellow male congregants. Services couldn't even begin until there were ten men present (a *minyan*).

Like other women in our congregation, my mother, sister, and I attended services, but we arrived late after getting lunch set up at the house. Then we would walk over to *shul*, where the men always started without us and the other women. After all, they didn't need us. Women had no role in the actual ceremony. Since we couldn't see or hear much, most of the women chatted throughout the proceedings anyway.

When my three older brothers turned thirteen, they had bar mitzvahs, commemorating their religious adulthood. They were welcomed into the community as full Jewish adults, got to perform in front of the entire membership, and were celebrated with a luncheon. When I turned thirteen, I had no such ceremony. In our religious community, girls did not have bat mitzvahs, the female equivalent of a bar mitzvah. Those were for *goyim*, my mother would say. While the term actually means "non-Jew," it's how our family referred to any Jews who were not practicing at our level of observance.

So, at a tender age, I gleaned that men were crucial to the practice of our religion—which was the center of our life. Women were not. Naturally, I was jealous of my brothers. I wanted to be up front, where I could see, hear, and learn. I wanted to be recognized as part of the community, too.

But the rules that barred me from these aims were well entrenched in our practice of Judaism. Who was I to question them, let alone alter them to fit my desires? So, every Shabbos throughout my childhood, I dutifully sat beside my mother in the back of the *shul*, unhappy with my lot, wanting more, and feeling powerless to do anything about my situation.

This changed as I approached the intersection of puberty, the women's rights movement, and relationships with some new friends I made in high school. These friends were unbound by the rules of Orthodox Judaism and were openly questioning traditional women's roles in the world. Because I lacked the education my brothers had, I didn't know the "why" behind the rules I lived by at home. It was very easy to question what I didn't understand to begin with.

Sure enough, over time, the dichotomy between who I was expected to be at home and in *shul* and who I was becoming at school and in my social group grew. I found I could no longer attend *shul* and sit silently in the back with my mother. So, I chose to not attend at all.

Though I wouldn't have known to express it back then, it was the first time in my life I didn't default to rules set for me by others (those thousands of years ago, no less). Instead, I chose my own path. Yes, this made things uncomfortable at home for a while—my parents were irritated with me and didn't make a secret of it. But I also had experienced a new kind of trust in myself from taking action to release a practice that didn't feel right and had been eating at me since before I could remember.

After putting myself through college and working for a couple of years, that trust in myself made another appearance. Against my parents' preferences, I chose to go to law school. My parents didn't like lawyers, didn't trust them. They hated that I had chosen the profession and said so vociferously.

I didn't know much about the law. At the time, I thought law school was a good choice for me and would lead to a solid, dependable, and lucrative career, all of which were important to me. I trusted in my own decision, despite my parents' lack of support. Little did I know of the orthodoxy and whole new set of archaic expectations awaiting me in the profession of law.

I was no stranger to hard work, but the amount law school required was insurmountable and seemed to be at cross-purposes with true learning for me. But I didn't question it. I did as law school dictated. I joined in the culture of study groups and all-nighters and no social life for a twentysomething. I assumed this was the path to graduation. And once I had my degree, I'd again have time to do the things I loved. So, I kept my head down, my mouth shut, and believed.

Right out of law school, I practiced civil litigation in private practice. I handled jury trials and all kinds of court appearances. The nature of the work and the hours required were relentless, just like law school. As were all associates, I was expected to be on constant alert, always at the ready, and poised for action. And I was.

Early in my career, I discovered there were "men's sections" in firms, too, except they're more like clubs. Not long into my tenure at one firm, all the attorneys—except me, the only female attorney— had been invited to a golf outing. Thinking it may have been an over-sight—inexcusable, but understandable—I naïvely brought this to the attention of a partner. I think because of the pall of sexism hang-ing over this particular situation, after thinking it over, he feigned ignorance of the oversight and invited me to the event. The feeling of exclusion was palpable the entire time I worked there.

Thinking firm culture was the problem, I changed jobs a few times. In one position, I worked for a boss who was a control freak. He monitored my every movement. The man decreed daily when I—a licensed, professional lawyer, not to mention an adult—could take a lunch break. Though I knew his behavior was wrong, I did not understand, at the time, how to do anything about it. Besides, I was too exhausted and too strapped for time to protest.

Moving forward, there simply would be too many incidents like this for me to push back on all of them—micromanagement, misog-yny, and misery seemed built into the private practice of law. As uncomfortable as it was and as wrong as it felt to me, I conformed to the reality of my situation and did my best to survive.

A decade and several law firms in, I was wearing out and having one stress-related illness after another—from plantar fasciitis in my feet to psoriasis on my scalp. One day my back started to hurt. By the end of that day, I couldn't stand up straight and would ultimate-ly spend the next month in bed lying flat on my back per doctor's orders.

For the first time since law school, I had time to myself to think. But all I could think about was work. Staring at the ceiling day after day, I worried about not being at work, while at the same time feeling relieved not to be there. I worried about having to give up law because of my physical condition, while at the same time being secretly delighted by the thought.

In truth, I loved practicing law but detested how it was practiced. Once again, the dichotomy between who I was inside and who an institution was expecting me to be was expanding. Once again, I found myself desperately unhappy with my lot, wanting more for myself, and feeling powerless to do anything about it.

I look back on that time and that person I was in amazement. I'd become so indoctrinated with the norms—the biases and the accepted expectations—of the profession that I couldn't imagine that law could be practiced differently. I didn't even consider whether the antiquated rules under which my firms (and most firms) operated was any way to run a business in the present day. The profession had raised me up—raised us all up—to believe that being stressed out at work and having strained personal relationships was the price to be paid if you want to make it in the legal profession.

CHANGING OUR COLLECTIVE STORY

I'd like to think this story of my early career in law is unusual. But it was not and is not. Many of my colleagues were living in misery right along with me. And many lawyers today—perhaps even you—are living out many of these same frustrations. It doesn't have to be like this.

Being overworked and overwhelmed is not a path to any kind of real or sustainable career or life. Far from it. No matter the mores of our profession, we are never without agency. It is more than possible to have a meaningful and satisfying career without being miserable, burning out, or selling out—even if your profession is law. You just have to know how. And this book will show you that.

While there was no national movement this time to wake me up to these truths, I was lucky enough to find a career coach who gave me the space to question the status quo in my profession. He didn't allow me to default to "the way it's done" or give in to the falsehood that "I can't do anything about it." He made me assess and define who I was, where I was, and where I wanted this career of mine to go—questions I'd never asked myself before. He made me see what was possible. Mostly, he dared me to be a full participant in my life—and that meant tapping back into that trust in myself, which had always reliably steered me in the right direction.

Guided by the framework my coach set out, I eventually and intentionally made the switch from private practice to government work. I decided on an in-house position in education law with the School District of Philadelphia. Working in government, especially on behalf of kids, was endlessly interesting and meaningful to me. Although we worked hard, the time demands were acceptable to me and thus manageable. For the first time since law school, I confidently bought concert tickets and went to the show without worrying about canceling because some last-minute assignment had been dropped on my desk. I'd found happiness as a government lawyer and particularly loved education law.

I later became general counsel to the Chester Upland School District and then chief counsel of the Pennsylvania Office of Open Records. During my time as chief counsel, I was regularly in the company of lawmakers, top-level government officials, and administrators. I testified before the Pennsylvania State Senate for funding, and we visited with members of the legislature to talk about the impact of the law on their constituents. Walking past the Pennsylvania Capitol building on my way to work and spending time in that beautiful building with its gorgeous and historic artwork never got old.

Adding to all this, I had a boss who appreciated me as a professional and employed my talents to their highest use—giving me real purpose, making me feel valued, and expressing confidence in my skill as an attorney. Terry L. Mutchler had been handpicked by the governor to run the Office of Open Records, which was brand-new. Step by step, Terry's mentoring and belief in me took me from being a respected behind-the-scenes strategist, too timid to appear in court, to having the skill and confidence to argue before the Pennsylvania Supreme Court.

The justices hated our case, and we lost. To me, though, making it to the position of lead in a state supreme court case was a huge win. That day, when I rose to speak, the courtroom was silent. The entire room was mine. I was no longer relegated to the back of a *shul* or chained to my desk because of some fossilized rule, with no voice of my own. No. I was standing in front of the Pennsylvania Supreme Court presenting an argument with everyone listening. I'd finally made it to the bema.

This career that provided me work I loved, that allowed me to grow both my skills and my influence as a professional, that provided me the life I wanted to live, didn't happen by accident, and it didn't happen by following standards someone else set out for me. It happened because I stopped defaulting to circumstances and started actively taking actions to determine my own life.

Yes, it was fortunate that government law was such a good fit for me, that I was promoted to the right position, and that Terry, of all people, ultimately became my boss. But if my choice of government law had turned out to be less than what I wanted for myself, I now had a framework, thanks to my coach, that I could return to and determine a better next move for myself and my career. I no longer had to put up with what an organization or firm chose to give me.

Between law school and actual practice, we attorneys get so caught up in and, I'd argue, exhausted by the demands of the profession, we come to believe we are without power to command our lives. The truth is I was never as stuck as I thought I was. And you aren't either, no matter your current circumstances.

In fact, several years after my state supreme court debut, I was again ready for a career change. I knew I had talent for helping colleagues cultivate their careers. I thought with my experience and insider knowledge, along with some additional training, I could help fellow attorneys avoid the misery so common in this profession and find their way to satisfying career and life.

TEN LAWS TO THE CAREER YOU WANT

As I've coached lawyers across the country over the last decade or so, I've seen that for the most part they are as unprepared to guide their own careers as I was when I graduated from law school in 1988. The client stories in this book represent those of the actual clients, with personal details altered. In many cases, these are composite stories. They, too, felt the tension between who they are deep down and who their workplaces were asking them to be. Helping those who practice law to resolve that tension and have the life and career they see for themselves is why I became a coach and why I wrote this book.

I talk to clients every day who wonder if practicing law ever gets less life-consuming, if it's possible to be an accomplished lawyer and also have time for family, friends, and maybe even themselves. At the same time, my clients are coming to the realization that earning a law degree and securing a job are only the first two pieces of building that career they once dreamed of. Yet, they aren't quite sure what other pieces they need, where to find them, or what to do with them once they have them.

There's a reason for this. For all our education, no one prepares us to build a career that meets our needs and preferences. Quite the opposite. As law students and then in practice, you (like me) were groomed to follow the status quo and hope it took you where you wanted to go, if you even knew where that might be.

From my own experience and from working with clients, I now have developed a framework like the one I used so many years ago, and it's specific to a career in law. This set of ten laws—laws no one ever taught us in law school—has taken hundreds of my clients and their careers from default to design. With each one building on the next, these laws will help you to regain that trust in yourself to know what is best for you, to figure out what a career of your own design might look like, and to give you the skill sets and tools to realize it. You will find these laws—all ten of them—laid out in the following pages, complete with suggestions and exercises to put your insights, skills, and practices to work for you right now and for the rest of your life.

If you are where I was so many times in my own life—unhappy with your lot, wanting more, and feeling powerless to do anything about your situation—know that you've already taken the first step to changing that. All you have to do now is turn the page, use these ten laws as your framework, and begin your move away from the status quo, away from others' expectations for you, away from having a career and life by default. Your own bema is out there waiting for you. And, rest assured, it will be one of your own design.

You Are Here

> *"You can't go back and change the beginning, but you can start where you are and change the ending."*
> —C. S. Lewis

G retchen, a family law attorney in New Jersey, came to my lawyer-coaching practice in a state of desperation. She wanted to quit her firm and leave the practice of law. She was tired of dealing with client emergencies at all hours, a standard part of family practice. She was tired of her boss expecting her to drop everything at a moment's notice—often causing her to work until 10:00 p.m. to complete his new assignments while keeping her own caseload going. Now in her forties, Gretchen feared she'd waited too long to get out and was worried her options were limited. She felt trapped.

When another client, Stacy, signed on for coaching, she'd already made partner in her boutique Maryland firm, thanks to her knack for attracting clients. Now she was being promoted to managing partner and felt she needed management skills. While she was proud of the promotion, she was also conflicted. As she described it to me, the job of managing partner didn't have "real teeth"—it was only a title and didn't come with any authority to act autonomously.

Not to mention, it would require countless unbillable hours doing firm administration work. When would she have time to expand her client book, which she regarded as the only true job security a lawyer had? But managing partner was a step up, and it's where her hard work had led. She'd be crazy not to take the promotion, right? She felt confused, especially as others weighed in on her good fortune.

I also remember a litigator who cried every Sunday night because she didn't want to go back to work on Monday. She'd made the decision to go to law school so she'd have a dependable career and a big paycheck. Now here she was, nearly a decade in, secure but hating her job. She felt stuck. By the way, that litigator was me.

There isn't a lawyer in practice who hasn't come to a crossroads in their career—not sure how they got where they are and even less sure of how to get where they want to be, or even where that is.

The reason why is simple. Most of us have never stopped to ask ourselves what we want from our law career, what we expect it to deliver for us. We don't think we get a say in what our life looks like—somewhere along the way we were taught our job determines that. We go from college to law school to the first opportunity that comes our way, and then one thing leads to another—until we find ourselves restless in our current position and unsure of what to do about it.

The crossroad may look different for each of us. Some of us, like Gretchen, stand at this intersection overwhelmed by the demands of the profession. We've fallen into a state of ennui as obligations mount and we get further behind in our work. Some of us, like Stacy, have good instincts about where our talents lie and the kind of career we want. But we feel pressured by expectations to go in the direction our higher-ups and professional traditions dictate.

Some of us love the law part of practicing but are perplexed by the business part—marketing, administration, human resources, and the like. No one in law school ever explained that a private practice was really a business, requiring skills beyond any you learned in your formal law education.

And still more of us, like me all those years ago, find ourselves several years into the profession feeling frustrated because we don't like what we're doing and can't seem to get ahead in the way we want. On one hand, we fear losing our job. On the other, we fear being in the same position, doing the same uninspiring work for two or three more decades.

DEFAULT VS. DESIGN

Whatever the exact circumstances that brought you to your particular crossroads, that constant restlessness and frustration that led you here stem from not being in control of your own life. Others are dictating your circumstances: what you do every day; how many hours you work (which determines your personal life); and whether and how your career advances. Unless you work for an organization whose mission is to help you have the career of your dreams—and my guess is you do not—you'll always be on track to achieve your organization's vision for itself, not your vision for you.

The choice before you and all of us in this situation is the same: either we continue the default pattern we're in—letting our career happen to us—or we take back our agency and commit to a career we design.

Maybe you are thinking that sounds great—a career by design. But you have student loans, a mortgage, and a family depending on you. You can't afford to quit your job and chase a dream. Or, you think designing a successful career is for those hard chargers who need to be at the top of the heap, and you're not like that.

Some of my coaching clients, to be sure, have bold, aggressive personalities, and a desire to make a lot of money and a name for themselves. By far, though, the majority are attorneys who want to find a way off the hamster wheel they're on. They want to do work that feels meaningful to them. They want to be of service to their clients. They also want to have time for a life outside the office, and they wonder if it's even possible to practice law and have a life.

It is possible. I know because I took my own law career from default to design, resulting in a practice that gratified me beyond any vision I'd had in law school. And now as a coach to lawyers, I've helped hundreds of attorneys—including Gretchen and Stacy—create the career in law and life they desire.

HOW YOU GET THERE

A career by design doesn't require that you become some overbearing, me-first career crusader. It doesn't mean that you don't do a great job for whatever firm or organization you work for now. It certainly doesn't ask that you quit your current job—at least not without a thoroughly considered reason and calculated next steps that advance your vision for your career and yourself.

What a designed career does ask is that you take the time to know what you want and what you value, and what your skills and expertise are. It asks that you then use that clarity to craft and follow a strategy to realize your vision. It requires you to become self-aware; to work at continual personal and professional development; to learn to recognize, mine for, and seize opportunity; and to take responsibility for where your career is headed.

While you don't have to be a big extrovert—though if you are, that's fine, too—you do have to be motivated. Transformation requires effort. And going from default to design requires both professional and personal transformation. You also need patience and faith. Such a change doesn't happen in an instant. The way forward won't always be obvious or smooth. The payoffs for your investment are rarely immediate. Moving your career from default to design is more of a slow build, as most worthwhile pursuits are.

The laws in this book provide you with the framework for that steady, sure build toward a career of your own design. Through the insights, strategies, and practices they offer, you learn to take charge of your career's direction, release the frustration of your current circumstance, and come to regard success as something you define for yourself. One law at a time, each supporting the next, you build the infrastructure necessary to achieve and maintain the career you want. All along the way and into your future, these laws keep you in touch and aligned with your values and your vision.

You are a professional. You have invested a great deal of time, money, and effort into who you are and what you have to offer. Just as important (if not more so), you are a person with a life of your own who gets to choose how that life is lived. The world deserves to have the best expression of you, and you deserve to have a career and a life that are everything you want them to be. These laws will take you there.

Your career is in your court now.

Law 1

Assess the Situation

> *"Knowing yourself is the beginning of all wisdom."*
> —*Aristotle*

You can't have the career you want until you know what you want. This means knowing what a successful career and life look like to you, not what they look like to your parents, your friends, your fellow lawyers, or society at large. To you. So, the first law of changing your career trajectory from one of default to one of your own design is *assess the situation*.

A satisfying career occurs at the intersection of personality (who you really are) and position (the requirements of the job). You must assess both to get the right fit for you.

TAKING STOCK

I was twenty-seven when I graduated from law school. I didn't have a clue about my "career path." That phrase wasn't even part of my vocabulary. In fact, there had never been a time when I seriously considered what I wanted to do or accomplish in life.

By default, I gravitated toward a clerkship at a litigation firm. Is that what I wanted to do? No clue. When they offered me a full-time position, I took it, thinking the hard part of my life was over. I was now a lawyer and could finally buy a car and rent a decent apartment. For a kid from a big family where money had been scarce, that was enough—at first.

By my mid-thirties, however, I was miserable. Litigation was all about money. While I appreciated a steady paycheck, money didn't hold much interest for me beyond that. All my colleagues talked about was how much money they brought into the firm, how much they made, what kind of car they drove, and the fancy clubs they joined. Patek Philippe watches, Tiffany cuff links, Porsches, Armani suits, and other status symbols signaled their value to each other. Litigation and all its trappings motivated them, which was great. For them.

Litigation left me hollow at the end of the day. The job, as I summed it up, was about transferring money from one person's pocket to another. However, this area of law was all I knew. I didn't see a way out. Thus, the tears every Sunday night.

Somewhere in the midst of my litigation misery, I was introduced to a career coach who had me assess myself and my situation, with an emphasis on my personal values. I quickly came to see that what I personally prized and what litigation rewarded were polar opposites. I realized that someone who doesn't like sending food back in a restaurant probably shouldn't be a litigator.

So, I researched jobs in areas of law more attuned to my values and my personality—which seems like common sense but had never occurred to me before. Using the data from my assessments, I made an informed decision to step off the partner track and step away from private practice altogether. I took a significant pay cut to become assistant general counsel to the School District of Philadelphia.

While some of my litigation firm colleagues may have seen this as a spiral down the drain, for me, it was a geyser. I got my life back. I was a satisfied lawyer. Not that it was an easy job; it wasn't. But it mattered to me, so I didn't mind the hard work.

Assessments don't change who we are; they simply reveal it. This allows us to make better choices. They uncover blind spots and expose what's important. They shine a light on the truth of ourselves and our situation so we can find our way to where we want to be.

THE ASSESSMENT PROCESS

That's why transforming your career from default to design begins with assessment (i.e., data collection)—unearthing your inner wisdom, recalling moments of flow and exhilaration, and using what you can learn from a variety of resources already within you.

I take all of my clients through a five-step assessment process—detailed below—that includes both personality and situational assessments.

Step 1: Select and take a formal personality assessment

Coaching clients sometimes resist discussing or looking at themselves in a personal way because they came to coaching for "business development" or some other official and business-y purpose. But the whole person comes to work, not just the work person. Your values, passions, preferences—the basic elements of your personality—don't change when you enter the office.

At its most simple, personality is like hair. You are born with a certain type, color, consistency, and so on. You can spend hours, dollars, and great effort in a salon manipulating it into something that represents your ideal look and end up with a style that requires a lot of ongoing management and never feels quite right. Or you can accept and appreciate your hair's natural qualities and find a style that looks great and doesn't require constant taming. In other words, you can squeeze yourself into an inappropriate role and be miserable, or you can expand yourself into a role that suits your true nature and so holds more satisfaction.

That's what assessment is all about: finding your fit.

In my practice, I administer the Hogan Personality Inventory—which is just one of many valid assessment tools out there. It assesses you across five broad dimensions of personality that are reportedly present in every socioeconomic group and every culture across the globe, no matter how primitive. Known as "the big five" or by the acronym OCEAN, the factors are:

- **O**penness to experience,
- **C**onscientiousness,
- **E**xtroversion,
- **A**greeableness, and
- **N**euroticism.

Whichever assessment tool you use, you'll want to make sure it includes these five factors because they provide a robust, layered, and nuanced understanding of your personality. You also want a tool that, like the Hogan, assesses motives, values, and preferences, giving you deeper insights into occupational preferences, what inspires and annoys you, and what you admire in others.

By identifying these things, you gain an understanding of your specific traits, both the bright side of your personality, when you are at your best, and the dark side, when you're triggered. Knowing your triggers gives you the ability to avoid them when possible. And when they are unavoidable, it allows you to create a plan to handle them more successfully. Having this data alone will reduce conflict at work and in your life.

A counselor, coach, or therapist can help you find the most effective personality assessment tool for you.

Step 2: Rate the eight domains of life

Work often becomes a convenient dumping ground for your personal life's complaints. The personality assessment tool allows you to separate true work issues from dissatisfaction in other areas of your life. This lets you know if it's really your job that needs changing or something else.

Once you've completed a formal personality assessment, take what you learn and use that data to rate the following eight areas of your life on a scale of zero to ten. Ten is highly satisfied, and zero is totally unsatisfied:

- Career
- Family and friends
- Significant other/romance
- Fun and recreation
- Health
- Money
- Personal growth
- Physical environment

After rating each life domain, take note of the low scores, where you're unsatisfied. Then tease out if the dissatisfaction in these areas might be creeping into how you perceive work and affecting your attitude toward it. For instance, maybe your boss isn't being unreasonable. Perhaps your teenager is driving you crazy, so your fuse is extra short at work these days.

Whatever the case, thinking this through moves you closer to identifying exactly what is bothering you and why. Then you can put your energy into improving what needs improving. You also create a truer state for seeing and evaluating any actual issues with your current job.

Don't assume that your lowest number requires the most immediate attention. Sometimes bringing an important area of life from an eight to a ten may be more meaningful to you.

Step 3: Log your time

Steps 1 and 2 drill down on who you are, what's important to you, and how satisfied you are with your life. Step 3—keeping a time log—lets you see in black and white if what you value and where you spend time are in alignment. I find my coaching clients are often surprised by the results.

For two weeks, keep a time log of everything you do—at work, at home, at play—and how much time you spend doing it. As Laura Vanderkam points out in her book, *168 Hours: You Have More Time Than You Think*, we each get 168 hours per week. You. Me. Beyoncé. Everyone. How you spend those hours makes all the difference.

Once you have that data, mine it. Are there places you waste time that you could reclaim? Are you giving time to something that isn't beneficial? Are you spending enough time on the activities and people that are important to you? Are you saying yes to things you don't want to do?

One client found this assessment tool personally powerful. Her log revealed she spent a lot more hours on childcare and household chores each week than her husband did, although they both had equally significant careers and income. When she sought to even this out, her husband's initial response was to compare himself with other husbands/dads who contributed far less. She observed that perhaps he should compare himself to her since they were running their house together. Armed with her logged data, she was able to confidently negotiate a more balanced distribution of work at home and get some time back to execute her other priorities.

Another client's log revealed that driving to work was a waste of her time. By taking the train instead, she reclaimed two hours a day—two more hours in which she could get some work done, listen to music, read a book, or just admire the scenery instead of gripping the steering wheel and grinding her teeth at the sight of traffic. This one simple change immediately made her life less stressful and more productive.

Step 4: Retrace your steps

When you were a kid and lost something, an adult probably told you to retrace your steps. What you've lost and are looking for in this exercise is your sense of direction where your career is concerned. And like any lost item, the best way to find it is to look at where you stand now and work backward.

In this step of your assessment process, you are going to think back over your entire career and identify and examine key decisions along the way. What you are looking for in each key moment is which of your impulses, instincts, fears, and desires worked for you and which didn't.

By examining past work situations and where they led, you can uncover which of your natural inclinations opened doors for you and pushed you toward things that fulfilled you and which ones took you in the wrong direction or held you back from opportunities. Note them. They are all important insights to have as you take charge of your career.

To help you gather this data, write out your answers to the following prompts:

- What made you choose your current work situation? What appealed to you then and now? What would you change?
- What did you envision when you graduated, and how does it compare with reality? Is the work you're doing what you

thought it would be? Did you make assumptions that didn't materialize? If so, what were they? And why didn't they materialize?

- Define any gap between how you wanted to feel about your career and how you do feel. (This is a great starting point for change.)
- What is draining your energy right now, and how can you minimize or eliminate it? (Reducing energy drainers is an essential step to creating time and space in your life. I routinely ask coaching clients to name five things that are currently taking away energy—answers have ranged from "my sister" to "spending too much time on social media.")
- Observe and document your responses to things at work, especially situations or assignments you find appealing and those you don't. What do you want more of? Less of? Be aware that we tend to focus on the things that bother us and gloss over positive things. (If you've ever given or received a performance evaluation, you know what I mean.) By being careful to document here rather than dramatize, you get a truer measure of how bad or good things really are for you. Every response should be regarded as information, pointing you toward or away from situations and circumstances. You are the anthropologist in your own life, observing what works and what does not.
- Create a timeline of your life and identify some peak experiences. Think about how each peak experience made you feel. Write it down. Who were you in those moments? Use the timeline to figure out how and why you created or chose your current situation. Let it remind you of your inner strength, as well as your ability to adapt and grow and create new peak experiences with an understanding of their significance to your development. Clients often recall long-forgotten moments,

accomplishments, and skills when they do this exercise, and that instills confidence. Whatever you've done before, you can do again.

And one more thing: don't run away from any feelings that come up as you move through this step or in life. There's data in our emotions. So, explore them. In 2005, I saw the movie *In Her Shoes*, about an unhappy Philadelphia lawyer who leaves her law career and becomes a dog walker while she figures out what to do next. I was an unhappy Philadelphia lawyer at the time. Sitting in the dark movie theater, I felt exposed. The movie tapped into that thing I suppressed, that thing I ignored, that thing I knew but didn't want to accept. When that happens to you, notice it. You don't have to do anything immediately. Just notice and remember. Also, keep a journal. That's more data.

Step 5: Assess your work situation

Now that you have a good amount of data on you and how you came to be where you are, you're ready to assess your current work environment. Ask yourself the following and write out your answers:

- What are the values in your workplace? Are they aligned with what you now understand is important to you? Differing values are the cause of much conflict at work and at home.
- Is there a mismatch between your values and strengths, and what you do at work? Many people spend hours doing things they hate or trying to be something they're not. Consider the possibility of such a mismatch when looking for the nature and cause of your discontent.
- Do you have what you need to be successful? If not, what could you ask for that may help? Do you need some training? Mentoring? Coaching? Identify some strategies and determine if they're offered or available where you currently work.

- Is staff support adequate? Sometimes firms refuse to proper-
  ly staff the office and expect lawyers to pick up the slack, doing
  their own typing and filing. That gets in the way of billing hours
  and building a book of business. If that's the case, it has to be
  addressed before you can ever operate at your optimum potential.

- Are you doing work that belongs to someone else? Despite
  having staff, many lawyers do work beneath their pay grade
  because they don't want to seem superior. I get it. My mother was a secretary and derisively referred to herself as a
  "secre-turkey." She felt her role wasn't important, even though
  it was critical. When I became a lawyer, I found it hard to ask
  support staff to do things I technically could do. But whether
  you are capable is beside the point. That is not what you've
  been hired to do. You're wasting both your time and the firm's,
  not to mention you are taking your staffer's job from them.
  How will they progress? You can't meet the demands of your
  job if you're unable to delegate—and that will cause frustration and poor productivity right there.

- Is leadership present and effective? Many lawyers work in
  rudderless organizations. There's nothing to buy into or follow, except financial distributions. Law firms are often com-
  prised of solitary silos, where the lawyers can't even cross-sell
  because they don't talk to each other or understand each other's practices. For some, this can lead to disenchantment and
  a desire to have more connection in their work lives. For rainmakers, it can also be an income-limiting roadblock.

- Do you feel respected, appreciated, and valued by the organization? As you know from your values exploration, this won't
  be important to everyone. For some, it is all about the money,
  and they are happy as long as there is lots of it. But if recognition and respect are things you'd like more of, workplace
  culture that provides those things may be a better fit.

- Do work expectations allow time for outside pursuits, such as family, exercise, and friendships? Many lawyers report they "don't have a life." Not having a life is no way to live. Perhaps you are assuming that deadlines are not negotiable when they might be. Or it could be that the hours required by your job are a deal breaker when it comes to your happiness and satisfaction. You won't know that unless you are willing to explore options and have conversations about what's possible.

When you have completed your situational assessment, take time to sit with your answers, and mine them for insights and direction. Keep them close so you can refer to them as we move through each law in this book. Let your discoveries and "aha!" moments from each step of the assessment process inform your thinking as you step into your new role as career designer.

IN ASSESSMENT THERE'S POWER

Like I had been, both Gretchen and Stacy from the opening section of this book were profoundly changed by what they uncovered about themselves and their situations through assessment.

Gretchen, the overwhelmed family practice lawyer, learned from her assessment that she was a people pleaser, which brought her to the life-changing insight that her "overwhelm" at work was more about her than her boss and clients. She never said no to anything.

With that information, Gretchen set a goal for leaving work by six o'clock every day and put some boundaries in place to make sure it happened. She had her assistant screen client calls, so Gretchen now only responded to true emergencies. When her boss appeared at her door with an unexpected task, she now said, "I can't do this and what I'm already working on in one day." And he now told her which assignment, if any, was the priority—which he would have been happy to do in the first place. The expectation that Gretchen needed to get the work done before she went home each day was hers, not his.

With those few changes, Gretchen was able to navigate her way to free up time for herself. She became happier and happier at her work. Family law—helping couples sort their issues—fit her values and personality. She'd come to coaching determined she needed to leave the practice of law and she finished coaching determined to stay.

Gretchen wrote to me several years later to let me know how much better her life had become. She reflected on how unhappy and overwhelmed she was before coaching, which caused her to lose sight entirely of how much she loved being a lawyer. As she took control of her life, Gretchen received multiple promotions and raises, and her life changed entirely to one that she designed and loved. The promotions and raises are proof that saying no at work is not career-ending. Quite the opposite. When Gretchen drew boundaries, everything improved, including her status at the firm.

But the biggest lesson in Gretchen's story is that if she'd left the law without knowing where the problem had been all along, she'd have taken those same people-pleasing tendencies to her next situation—inevitably ending up overwhelmed once again.

And the world would have lost a phenomenal, caring, compassionate attorney. Great lawyers leave the law every day because of working conditions, but some leave because they don't understand how to negotiate and modify them.

Stacy, who was up for that promotion to managing partner, also found the assessment process invaluable. It showed her to be socially self-confident and competitive. She enjoyed being in the spotlight, and in the workplace, she could be tough, direct, and blunt. That combination could be a problem for a manager or team leader but was a huge strength for business development and marketing. She was a natural at entertaining clients, was an excellent negotiator, and was resilient when it came to the rejection that comes with sales.

Firm leadership was leading Stacy in a direction that didn't speak to her. She wanted to be a rainmaker. Could she have done the managing partner job? Yes. She may even have done it well, but she would have felt restricted and unable to use her true talents. Supported by what she learned through assessment, Stacy declined the managing partner role and chose to focus on business development, the path that aligned with her strengths, values, and preferences.

A few years after she made this decision, larger and more prominent firms began actively recruiting Stacy, leading her to even more lucrative opportunities than would have ever appeared if she were busy at the helm of a firm.

As for me, I thrived as a government lawyer. In ten years' time, I rose through the ranks to become chief counsel to a commonwealth agency. As much as I loved it, when I hit the twenty-year mark, I was ready for a change once more, this time outside the practice of law. Again, I used assessment to help me choose and then design my second act as a coach for lawyers.

Assessment made it possible for Gretchen, Stacy, and me to step into a new level of power when it came to determining our careers and lives. That's what taking the time to figure out who you are, what you want, and where you are now can do for you. It's why your quest to take charge of your career and your life begins with assessment.

Our personalities can either interfere with or support our goals. If you are dissatisfied with the status quo, there are reasons. Assessment allows you to uncover what they are. So, whenever you find yourself asking, "How did I get here?" you'll know to turn first to assessment.

LAW 1 IN BRIEF

- Assessment (knowing yourself and your situation) is the first step to having a career by design.

- Assess yourself. Choose a formal, valid assessment tool that measures the five big dimensions of personality (OCEAN), as well as your motives, values, and preferences. Then apply what you learn to the eight domains of life.
- Assess your career journey thus far. Use the assessment tools in this chapter to look at where you are, how you spend your time, and what worked and what didn't along the way.
- Assess your situation. Use the assessment tools in this chapter to evaluate your current work environment. Use the data you collect to inform your design of the ultimate work environment for you.
- Keep notes on all the data you collect. You will use it as you move through the remaining nine laws to become the designer of your career.

Law 2

Investigate Before
You Commit

> *"It is a capital mistake to theorize before one has data."*
> *—Sherlock Holmes in Sir Arthur Conan Doyle's*
> A Scandal in Bohemia

Clients often feel eager for immediate change after their personal and situational assessments are complete. Understandably so. Now that they have an idea of what direction to go, they want to strike out on that path right away. While I encourage their newfound enthusiasm and agency, I caution against taking any action without first knowing what this new path really looks like, what is involved in taking it, and what you are likely to find once you're on it—the positives as well as the challenges. Which all boils down to Law 2: Investigate Before You Commit.

Unexamined decisions are usually how we land in a job or even a life that doesn't quite fit. Successfully shifting from default to design in your career means slowing down your decision-making process, gathering information, and then using that intel to think and act strategically.

When Patrick came to coaching, he was a professional malpractice litigator, largely representing individuals and companies being sued for financial advisor negligence, fraud, and misconduct. Patrick had been unhappy for years in his position in the Florida office of a national law firm. Fully aware he was following a career path that didn't suit him, he told me, "Shortly after I took the job, I realized I didn't want to practice law—at least, not this way. But the salary was good, I had a family to support, and it's what I knew. So, I stayed on the path of least resistance."

Now nearly two decades down that path, the daily grind had become so painful for Patrick that he was ready to take off in a new direction, whatever was required of him. He was bogged down in frustration and felt the need to move forward. He couldn't bear the thought of spending another twenty years miserable in his work. Though he wanted desperately to reinvent himself professionally, he wasn't sure how and dedicated himself to figuring it out.

Patrick knew from his assessment that he had scored high on the altruism scale, which indicates a strong motivation to help others, and in security (meaning that he needs stability in his work). His profile also revealed a characteristic ubiquitous among lawyers I've tested—low adjustment, characterized by anxiety and low resilience. Low-adjustment people don't respond well to sudden changes in plans. They are self-critical, edgy, and tense. On the positive side, they work very hard to overcome any deficiencies and want to do a good job.

Patrick's adjustment score explained why he had been so uncomfortable with the unpredictability, stress, and acrimonious nature of litigation.

As Patrick thought about his next steps, he concluded that he would most likely do better in a role with fewer crazy curveballs—so maybe a smaller law firm would be best. He thought he might like a position where he could be of service, and one that offered stability, structure, and a clear path to earning a stable income.

As we explored various avenues, Patrick shared that a particular pain point for him in his current job was that so many of the cases he defended were brought by victims of bad financial advice from so-called professional advisors—advice so bad some had grounds to seek damages. He was incensed that good people had to go through the cost and demands of a legal proceeding to reclaim what they had worked their whole lives to secure. He confided that he'd been thinking about the financial industry for years and thought he might like to do what he could to prevent people from losing their money in inappropriate investment schemes in the first place. Patrick was thinking of giving up the law altogether to become a financial advisor.

The more Patrick talked, the more gung-ho he became about opening some kind of financial planning services firm. He began talking about getting certification, the different types, who he imagined his clients would be, and where he might look for office space. As excited as he was and as good as it all sounded, before enrolling in a course or making any big moves, he needed to investigate before he committed—aka Law 2.

Investigating would allow Patrick to fully grasp what being a financial advisor entailed, not just on paper or in his imagination. Done well, an investigation would educate him fully as to what such a career change would require of him. With this knowledge, Patrick could better judge if it really was the right move for him right now—before he invested significant time and effort and risked his income.

THE INFORMATIONAL INTERVIEW

The most efficient way for Patrick—and you—to gather such information on a career option is an "informational interview." It's a tool I learned about when I made the shift from default to design in my own legal career. Simply put, you find someone who is already doing what you think you might want to do and get the inside scoop from them. You let them educate you on the reality of the job—the upsides as well as the downsides. Through this awareness, you can make better choices and better prepare for whatever direction you choose to take your career.

Just like Patrick, I was once a lawyer looking for a way out of my litigation practice. Unlike Patrick, however, my first thought was that health care law might be the right fit for me. After all, I began my career as a personal injury attorney. In order to prove my cases, I had to understand the cause, nature, significance, and duration of physical or psychological injuries, as well as any impairment resulting from them. Over the years, I became well versed in many complex bodily processes. I pored over medical records, cross-examined medical experts, and created successful outcomes through my burgeoning medical knowledge. This work also led to deep understanding of the workings of the insurance industry and risk management. I thought I could just pivot my expertise toward something that would not involve jury trials. Perhaps a career as a health care attorney? That sounded good. On paper.

To confirm my notions, and at the suggestion of my career coach, I sought out a practicing health care attorney and set up an informational interview. All it took was a few minutes of conversation to know that was not the area of law for me.

What I imagined the practice of health care law to be and its reality were two very different things. By the health care attorney's own description, the majority of that kind of law is transactional—negotiating and drafting contracts. I'd chosen litigation in the first place because drafting legal instruments held zero interest for me. Same thing with entertainment law. It sounded interesting and exciting, but it turned out to be largely contracts.

It really pays to take a good look under the hood of a potential career. If I had not taken that time to talk with that lawyer, my naïve self may have forged ahead with health care law. I may have sailed through the interview process, committed to a firm, and within a year found myself miserable once again.

Mystery writer Louise Penny's famous character (and a favorite of mine), Chief Inspector Armand Gamache, tells all new police recruits that there are four sentences to use for acquiring knowledge: "I was wrong. I'm sorry. I don't know. And I need help." It's true. Much can be learned by using these sentences. By investing a quarter of an hour in asking for help, the informational interview can let you know in no uncertain terms if an area of law is wrong for you, which then frees you to keep searching for the right one.

CONDUCTING AN INFORMATIONAL INTERVIEW

Some of my clients balk at the idea of calling a lawyer they don't know and asking for a meeting. They say things like: "Time is money to lawyers." "No one wants to take time out of their day to talk to me." "Why would they do it? There's nothing in it for them." If these phrases are rolling around in your head right now, I remind you that law is a profession built around supporting our fellow lawyers. If someone called you and asked if they could talk to you about your area of practice, my guess is you would not only say yes, but you would also be flattered they thought you were an expert worth consulting.

When you ask for help, know that it taps into something in other people that makes them feel good. Worst-case scenario, they say no, and you move on to the next person on your list.

Once you identify a career direction you would like to investigate, here are the steps to setting up and conducting informational interviews:

1. Identify people who are currently in a role that interests you. This can be someone you know, have heard of, or found through research. LinkedIn is a great place to find interview candidates. The platform allows you to search by job title, then prompts you to filter by jobs, people, or groups. A heads-up, though, when you search by "title": you are likely to get a list of hundreds of thousands of people with that title. You may want to filter by connections, organizations, or groups, or begin with a firm or company and then find affiliated people.

2. Contact several of the people your research has identified and request fifteen minutes of their time. Send them a short message that includes the reason for the meeting (you are interested in their field), mentions why you chose to reach out to them particularly (what about them impressed or inspired you), and lets them know you won't take more than fifteen minutes of their time. Also, make it clear you're not looking for a job.

3. When they say yes, take the initiative and set everything up. If you are meeting online, create the meeting and a calendar invite. If it is by phone, again, create a calendar invite with all the information and make clear that you'll initiate the call. Make sure the date, time, and process is clear.

4. Before your scheduled meeting, learn everything you can about the person and their company or firm—where they went to school, prior positions held, social media posts, interests, and passions.

5. Draft targeted questions for the interview. Follow journalism's "inverted pyramid" principle: list your most important

questions first and go from there. Some reliable questions to ask include, What interested you about your field? Is the work what you thought it would be? What was your path to where you are now? Tell me about a day in the life in your work—what do you spend time doing on a regular basis? What are a few things you like about it? And what don't you like? What questions should I be asking about the industry or role? What do you wish you had known before taking your current role or joining the industry?

6. At the meeting, begin by introducing yourself and teeing up the point of the meeting (e.g., "I've been a litigator for ten years, specializing in insurance defense, and am considering going in-house, like you. I'd like to ask you a few questions about the field and your experience in it.") Keep the description of yourself short. You already know about you. You want to know about them. Always remember, this isn't a job interview, so avoid the temptation to sell yourself.

7. Make sure you don't go over the promised fifteen minutes, unless the other person is prolonging the conversation. You can say something like, "I want to be respectful of your time and not go over." You will know from the response whether it's time to wrap up or if they'd like to speak a little longer.

8. Immediately after the meeting, send a personalized, handwritten, thank-you note to show you appreciate their time. Handwritten notes acknowledge that a person went out of their way in a manner unique to emails and texts. If you met at their office, send it there, and if you don't have a physical address, an email is the next best way to say thank you.

After the meeting, make detailed notes. Writing not only gives you a record to look back on with details you may forget, but it also helps you process what was discussed. As you write, keep your personal assessment in front of your mind and be sure to sketch out what aspects of the job are a good fit for you and what aspects might be a challenge or a deal breaker.

Before jumping into any financial advising courses, Patrick conducted informational interviews with professional stockbrokers, money managers, insurance experts, certified financial planners, and investment advisors. With each interview, he realized more and more what a risky business money management is—even if you're giving sound advice.

In addition, he learned that while the field offered plenty of potential to make money, he could expect his income for the first few years to be uneven at best. He would also have to go back to school to earn certification. While this emotionally appealed to him (he'd scored high in learning approach in his assessment and loved academic pursuits), practically, it would lengthen the time it would take to build a clientele and a steady income. With a family to support, that wouldn't be optimal.

Most important, Patrick saw that a day in the life of a financial advisor was not so different from a day in the life of a lawyer—though not a litigator, involved in conflict all day long. It was closer to transactional law, proactively helping clients avoid problems, rather than reactively helping to fix them.

Somewhere in the middle of these interviews, Patrick ended up in a conversation with an estate-planning attorney. When that attorney began talking about his business—the services he offered and the issues he was able to handle for clients—Patrick was intrigued and excited. He could see that area of law would allow him to help people avoid financial catastrophe with proper planning and, at the same time, permit him to practice law in a way he'd enjoy it. Best of all, he could see that such a practice would offer a more reliable income stream—providing Patrick and his family a comfortable level of security.

Adding to the positives, the ramp-up to success would not take as long as financial planning would, and best of all, estate planning could provide a fairly regular schedule and more predictable routine than a litigation caseload.

Patrick had extensive contacts and connections in the Florida legal scene where he was already practicing, and was regarded as a good lawyer. He was active in the local bar, sat on a few boards, and knew many lawyers who could refer estate-planning work to him. The aging demographic in his particular location meant there were lots of potential clients needing estate-planning services.

As another bright spot, Patrick needed no additional formal education to begin practicing in this area of the law—though he'd still get to indulge his love of learning with a combination of self-teaching and continuing legal education courses in estate planning. He could see exactly what he needed to do to grow his skills and expand the services he would offer.

After much consideration and more research, Patrick chose to start his own estate-planning law firm. Although he thought about working for another firm first, Patrick knew he wanted to be his own boss and was confident in his ability to run the office, generate business, and learn what he needed in order to help his clients.

LOOK BEFORE YOU LEAP

When looking for "next moves," the majority of us lawyers aren't looking to go out on our own, although some have the entrepreneurial spirit required to handle cases, run the office, and be the rainmaker, too. Getting a law firm off the ground is a complex endeavor. If that's your trajectory, you need to do research and look at what various firms have to offer, analyze the competition, and create some differentiators for your practice. Data makes the difference between a career by default and one by design. So, you want to apply the same rigor to investigating organizations of interest as you did to looking into the career direction you've chosen.

If you know which firms or companies you'd like to join, dive into researching them. If you are having issues finding organizations of interest, consider contacting an executive search firm or a legal recruiter. They will know where to look. In addition, recruiters can be a valuable source of up-to-the-minute workplace trends, résumé tips, and networking guidance. Keep in mind that recruiters are busy, too, and keep your questions crisp and targeted. Finally, research organizations that align with your values. Create saved alerts, and check the online job boards of organizations you're interested in, as openings are not always advertised on employment websites.

Remember, everything that has brought you to this point is in play. Once you have a list of entities worth looking into, employ these three steps in your investigation:

Step 1: Collect all the background you can on the organization

- Review company websites for things that are important to you. Does the organization have a mission statement? Diversity? Enunciated values that resonate with yours?
- Check company profiles on LinkedIn, Facebook, and other social media platforms.
- Use search engines and YouTube to find articles, videos, and information on various organizations and anyone from them you'll be meeting.
- Check out websites, such as Glassdoor.com, where users post anonymous reviews and salary information on many organizations.
- Search the news and business journals for mentions of the company or people involved.

- Check the Bureau of Labor Statistics for industries, occupations, and earnings.
- Look for lists of great places to work. Go to www.greatplace towork.com and www.glassdoor.com for information and reviews on organizations. And look to publications like *Fortune* or *Forbes* that do regular roundups of best places to work.

Step 2: Identify which organizations look best for you. Cull your list. And move in a little closer.

- See if you know anyone who works at the organizations you are considering. Or who used to work there. By speaking to a current associate at a firm I was considering, I avoided walking on board a sinking ship. Thank goodness for intelligence (data) and connections.
- Check to see if any of your LinkedIn connections have an affiliation. Did they used to work there? Or have friends who still work there?
- Use LinkedIn to directly search for people who work at the company—most list contact information.
- If you find a connection, ask for an introduction.

Step 3: Make contact

- When you find a firm or organization you might like to work for, use the contacts you've made to explore how to position yourself for a role there.
- If you don't have a direct contact or see another way in, return to your research. Find out who you need to talk to and reach out.
- When you get an interview, remember this is a two-way street. You are assessing the organization and role as much as they are assessing you. This is about you finding the right fit for

you, a place that advances your vision for your career. Use the knowledge you gathered from your assessments and your informational interviews to create questions that give you the information you need to make the best decision for you.

DEAL BREAKERS VS. RED FLAGS

As you evaluate the data from your investigation to determine what you might want to commit to, remember that no job, organization, or career path is going to be a perfect fit with your values, preferences, and current skill set. So, don't expect it to be. As you weigh which next step to take, consider which of the ill-fitting aspects of any particular career path constitute deal breakers and which are simply red flags.

Deal breakers are aspects of the job where the effort to overcome them far outweighs your desire to head in that direction (for Patrick, as an uninitiated financial planner, his immediate prospects were a deal breaker). Red flags, on the other hand, are still obstacles, to be sure, but perhaps worth the effort to overcome. Whatever direction you decide to go, you'll want to be aware of the red flags (and there will always be red flags) and figure out how best to mitigate them.

For Patrick, making the decision to have his own firm didn't automatically eliminate his aversion to risk or completely quell his anxiety. He still found the idea of starting his own law firm daunting. Because he tended toward catastrophic thinking, Patrick often imagined worst-case scenarios and his assessment showed a moderate level of ambition (as defined by the Hogan scale). Don't you need high ambition to be CEO of your own law firm? These were red flags he'd need to work through. For his clients, though, Patrick's skill in imagining worst-case scenarios would help avoid them.

I felt some of the same things when I started my coaching business. Like Patrick, I scored low on the adjustment scale of the Hogan

Personality Inventory, meaning that while I am open to feedback, I am self-critical and do not tolerate stress as well as those who scored high. My ambition score was lower than Patrick's. Becoming a coach sounded great, but I was just as worried about getting the work and being CEO of my own company, as was Patrick.

Patrick, however, had prodigious positives in his profile that would enable him to overcome these red flags. He was warm, genuine, caring, curious, funny, and immensely likable. As a hard worker, his intense interest in helping others would help him prevail over negative thinking and endear him to clients. His need for security, a goodly amount of interpersonal sensitivity and ease with networking would balance out any lack of drive when it came to marketing and procuring clients. His intelligence and love of learning would also see him through investigating and investing in technology and office management systems, as well as becoming comfortable in a new area of practice.

Once Patrick made the decision to have his own firm, his focus in coaching shifted from creating clarity to creating a plan. With self-awareness, he figured how and when to lean into his strengths. He learned to manage his fears and develop areas of weakness. And he made a lot of checklists. This helped Patrick feel grounded and provided daily and weekly evidence of his activity, commitment, and, yes, ambition.

Patrick took a full two years to leave his job and open his practice. When he did it, he had enough money socked away to make it for the first year if he kept expenses low. Today, happy with his choice and less stressed than when he was a litigator, Patrick would tell you that all the data collecting and preparation paid off in lowering actual risks, as well as his anxiety. Investigating before committing made taking this leap into a new career direction easier and surer than it would have been otherwise.

Whether you go out on your own or choose a new position in a new firm, you will have to lean into your strengths and manage your red flags and triggers as well. The more assessment and research you do up front, the more prepared you can be—and the more success you are likely to have.

A CAREER BY DESIGN IS A PROCESS

The road to transformation is not a straight one and cannot and will not be plotted out in its entirety early in the process—or ever, really. Neither Patrick's nor my career transformations took us where we initially thought they would. With every day comes new challenges and opportunities for your career—and you—to grow and change.

Especially when you are in the investigatory, data-gathering part of this process, be open-minded. It's a mistake to start your research with a long list of "must haves" and "can't dos." For the best result (the one that's going to uncover the best next step for you), set a simple goal of having awareness. Be prepared to question your long-standing beliefs and explore alternative ways of seeing things.

As lawyers, it is funny how much we focus on due diligence. Yet, when it comes to our own careers, we are so ready to leap. We want to run away from the bad, but toward what? The more data we have, the better and more effective decisions we can make about our careers. That is not to say that every decision or every step will be perfect. It won't be. But Law 2: Investigate Before You Commit gives you a process for evaluating what is going right, what is going wrong, and what next action makes the best sense for you.

With each iteration of this process, your vision for yourself becomes clearer and clearer, moving closer and closer to choosing a direction and creating the career that suits your talents and stirs your passions.

LAW 2 IN BRIEF

- Great design should not be rushed. Investigate before you commit.
- Conduct informational interviews with several professionals who are currently doing work you are potentially interested in doing.
- Research firms, companies, or organizations that do work you are interested in. Use information from your assessment to evaluate if their work environment is a good match for you.
- Before you interview with anyone, know the organization you are walking into and be prepared to ask questions. Remember, you are interviewing them as much as they are interviewing you.
- Sort all negatives into deal breakers and red flags by determining what is worth the effort to manage (red flags) and what isn't (deal breakers).
- Understand that a career by design is a process, not a destination. Start with an open mind and keep it that way.

Law 3

Don't Double Down on Past Decisions

> *"Insanity is doing the same thing over and over again and expecting different results."*
>
> —*Albert Einstein*

If we all grew up to do what we dreamed about in kindergarten, there would be a lot more ballerinas and firefighters in the world. But as we mature and learn more about the world and ourselves, our dreams change and our plans along with them. To carry out those new plans, we must make new decisions. Nobody questions that.

My guess is very few of us look back on the hours and hours we spent imagining ourselves dancing across a stage or driving a big red engine and consider it wasted time or a lost investment. We didn't stick with our kindergarten dreams out of some sense of false loyalty or label ourselves quitters because we didn't follow through on that original choice. And when, as preteens, we came across a career direction we felt held more promise (astronaut? veterinarian? paleontologist?), we certainly didn't throw up a wall of reasons why we couldn't change our minds and be who we wanted to be.

Somehow as we age, however, we don't give ourselves the same grace. Once we start creating a career path, many of us hesitate to veer from it—even though most of us were eighteen years old when we laid the groundwork for the path we are now trudging. I am sure some college freshmen were lucky enough to choose a major that led to a career that fulfills them to this day. But most of us at that age didn't even know who we were, let alone what work we might find satisfying ten years down the road. In my case, I didn't really know myself until I was in my thirties, and by that time, I was already a lawyer.

Given how little we know when we make these monumental decisions, it's no surprise that here we are now in a job or maybe even a field that doesn't quite fit. And instead of making a new decision, a course-correct that would put us on the career path we would choose today, we (and by that I mean most people) double down on our past decisions, playing mind games with ourselves to keep us there.

That brings us to Law 3: Don't Double Down on Past Decisions.

When a decision made in the past is no longer working, or never did, a big mistake people make is to dig in rather than change course. Regardless of how good these decisions were when you made them (e.g., specializing in an area of law that seemed promising, accepting a job with a paycheck that pulled you out of debt, or buying a low-mortgage fixer-upper), they now feel more like an obligation that keeps you from getting what you want from life. You feel trapped by that old decision. By continuing to honor it when you know it's not working, you make a new poor choice every day.

There are a host of reasons why we double down on past decisions, but most of those reasons are rooted in our very human aversion to change. Change comes with risk and uncertainty, both of which our brains are wired to avoid. Our brains perceive change as a threat. Thus, when challenged with a decision, our thought processes automatically push us toward whatever is needed to maintain the status quo—whether that status quo serves us or not. Our brains want to know what to expect more than they want happiness and fulfillment, as counterintuitive as that sounds. Change brings discomfort. Even though change is positive and the discomfort temporary, the brain sounds the alarm, which brings fear to the forefront of our thoughts.

This biology cannot be underestimated or overstated. But it can be dealt with. With awareness and a strategy, we can override and manage our default thinking to ensure our decisions are made by design.

EXPENDITURE VS. INVESTMENT

By far, the biggest driver of our doubling down on past decisions is a thought process known in economics as *sunk cost fallacy*—our very human penchant to stick with something simply because of the time, money, and/or effort we have already put into it. (Take notice, this tendency isn't limited to career choices. This resource waster haunts every aspect of our lives.)

Too many lawyers to count have come into coaching because they are miserable in their work and yet are hesitant to make a change. They say they can't just walk away from the "investment" they've made getting where they are—the cost of their legal education, the effort in securing their position, the time it has taken them to climb the organizational ladder, and so on.

I'd argue "investment" is the number-one reason clients give for doubling down on a decision that's no longer working for them. I'd also argue that those same clients are confusing the word *investment* with *expenditure*. We tend to treat those words as interchangeable. But doing that keeps us chained to the past and causes us to make decisions based on the wrong criteria.

The key difference between investment and expenditure is appreciation—meaning growth. An investment is capable of appreciation, expanding in value. An expenditure is not. An expenditure is just spent, gone. It doesn't grow, and you can't get it back.

When we treat an expenditure (time, money, effort) like an investment, we imbue it with loyalty and value it doesn't have and doesn't deserve. We're essentially saying that because we spent time, money, or effort doing something, that is where our growth opportunity lies. So, we think we must continue to do that same thing to keep our "investment" growing. This is demonstratively untrue.

The only thing that grows out of you staying in the wrong situation is misery. How many people do you know who choose to stay in the wrong marriage, job, or business based on time served (an expenditure)? There is no future benefit or profit in time served.

If you continue an endeavor believing it's going to "pay off" because of the number of resources you've already expended, you are sinking good resources into a bad situation based on a false expectation of a return. You are the hostage of sunk cost fallacy thinking. Previously expended resources are just that—expended.

Thinking of expenditures as investments closes your mind to other options, making you unable to recognize opportunity, let alone make a decision to seize it. Anything that cannot be recouped should not be part of your decision-making equation. How many hours, months, years, or dollars you've spent is irrelevant. Really. When you're miserable, what sense does it make to spend the rest of your life doing the same thing?

Sunk cost fallacy thinking keeps us in a default position. A career by design demands our decisions be based not on what we've lost and cannot get back, but on what we stand to gain.

THE COST OF SUNK COST FALLACY

Marjorie was a successful commercial litigator and partner in her Philadelphia law firm. A longtime client impressed with her work offered her an in-house position in a major financial institution. The job came with a substantial salary boost, lucrative incentives, and an opportunity to lead a legal department. She came to coaching to figure out what to do.

With every fiber of her being, Marjorie wanted to say yes to the opportunity right away. But she felt uneasy about leaving her current firm. She had been there for twenty years, her whole career. As she told the story, the firm had "invested" so much in her, and she too had "invested" so much in rising through the ranks to become partner. She didn't want to appear ungrateful for all they'd done for her. She felt she would be abandoning her partners if she took the job.

I presumed the intense loyalty Marjorie felt was due to something significant, something really big she got from the firm, something that was and would continue to add value to her career. Perhaps a partner had taken her under his wing, and she had more to learn. Or maybe the firm provided a path for professional development and further promotion she was wary about giving up. Or maybe, now that she was a partner, she would have a voice in shaping the firm's future, something she wanted very much.

As she continued to speak, however, she said nothing of the kind. With every word, it became clear she'd clawed her way to the top of that firm over her two decades there. And even though she was a partner now and serving on the executive committee, she still didn't have a voice. Her initiatives—and everyone else's, by the way—were ignored because all the control and power resided in one person. Any new ideas or chance for real leadership would have to wait until this person's retirement.

From her own description, there were no benefits associated with longevity at this firm. Like so many of us, Marjorie was operating under the false notion that working many years in a firm is an investment rather than an expenditure.

The truth was she had nothing more than a job that paid a salary. Neither side had any investment in the other; both were free to pull up stakes anytime. Loyalty to an employer does not require staying forever. Her only responsibility was to do a great job while she was there, and she had done that and then some. The score was even enough. Her resistance to handing in her notice was sunk cost fallacy thinking.

"So," I asked Marjorie, "what exactly makes you feel so loyal to these douchebags?" To be profane with a client was a gamble. I knew that. But sometimes with a buttoned-up client like Marjorie—a twenty-year corporate attorney from a conservative firm and deep into their story—being a little vulgar can loosen the guardrails and jolt her into a more real and candid perspective.

Marjorie laughed as if I'd said the funniest thing in the world. Then she got quiet. "I made my firm a lot of money over the years, but when I think about it, nothing was given to me. I made my own opportunities." There was relief in her voice. "I don't really have an obligation to them, do I?"

When Marjorie had received the offer to become in-house counsel, the only relevant consideration in her decision should have been her present circumstances: Which situation was better for her now? And for her family? How did the two jobs compare in terms of role, benefits, location, requirements, and compensation? Which was a better match for her preferences and desires?

Marjorie's personal assessment had shown her top values to be security, recognition, and power. She had a strong occupational preference for a role in an organization that offered stability, not volatility. She also wanted her contributions acknowledged and to be influential with a voice at the table.

Viewing the offer through the lens of her present circumstances, she easily saw that two of her three top values were unmet at her current firm, where her ideas were rejected and her accomplishments ignored. Her choice became clear. She followed her values right into a higher paying job as vice president and chief legal counsel for an organization where her voice would matter and her influence would be unlimited.

CHANGING YOUR RELATIONSHIP IN ORDER TO CHANGE

Some of us, however, don't even make it to sunk cost fallacy thinking. Just the thought of change, any change, overwhelms us. We shut down opportunity to shut out our anxiety. So, we never seriously consider what could be.

As with any situation that overwhelms, the way to work through this is to break down the potential change into more manageable pieces. Bite-sized chunks. This works exceedingly well for career changes because they typically aren't one big, sudden event. They are by their nature a process, a series of small events over time. Small changes, taken one at a time, are easier on the brain. Resistance even goes down as you progress.

Amy was by far the youngest partner in her suburban Maryland real estate and municipal land use firm. Her colleagues were nearing retirement, and so they were slowing down and not bringing new clients to the firm like they used to. However, they continued to be paid the same—which was more than Amy, who was bringing in a lot of new business. One partner, in fact, had reduced to part time that year and still took home a bigger paycheck than Amy.

Her partners' waning interest in the firm also meant waning support and resources for Amy. When she needed assistance on big deals, no one was around to lend their expertise or help. The harder she worked, the less her partners did—causing her frustration and resentment to grow.

Then out of the blue, a competing firm began recruiting Amy. At first glance, the new firm seemed to have everything her current firm did not. It was bigger, would pay more, handled larger deals, enjoyed a tremendous reputation, and was a more sophisticated practice.

Once they offered her a position, Amy did a little research and confirmed every one of the new firm's attributes. Still, she was hesitant to say yes. She'd been at her current firm for ten years. Though there was no evidence the conditions at her firm would get better, she told herself it would be okay. She felt comfortable there, she knew the routine, and she liked her partners, even though they'd disappointed her mightily in the last several years. The idea of leaving simply felt overwhelming for Amy. As she put it, "I can't imagine starting all over."

I could see Amy's brain was headed toward doubling down and maintaining the status quo, without fully weighing her options. Amy, more than most, did her best to dodge change whenever possible. As an introvert, she avoided people she didn't know, and she organized her life to steer clear of unfamiliar situations.

Whether or not she was conscious of it, thinking of going to a new firm with new people filled her with anxiety. It was not a thought her brain liked or wanted to entertain. So, it automatically went for "no," bolstered by the contorted reasoning that it was more comfortable to stay in a situation she knew—even though it meant more work, less pay, and continuing resentment and frustration. Based on her partners' relaxed attitudes, it wasn't clear how far into the future this firm would even go. There were significant risks in staying, but Amy wasn't focused on those. She was more focused on the risk of leaving because it would upset the status quo.

To interrupt her doubling down, untangle her reasoning, and at least give Amy the chance to seriously look at this opportunity, we needed to first bring Amy's default thinking into her consciousness. So, I asked her a similar question to the one I asked Marjorie (and in a similar tone): "Where the hell is this loyalty coming from, woman?"

Amy laughed and that relaxed her. It was enough to cause her brain to halt the automatic resistance to change and open enough to consider the real pros and cons of the choice before her.

To further ease her brain's anxiety, we broke her predicament down into the opportunity before her and her objections to it. Then we took it one consideration at a time. This both defused her discomfort and allowed for clearer thinking.

Through that clear thinking, Amy was able to remind herself that her top values (high interest in security and commerce) would be better served by the new job because of the firm's reputation and business. Her current firm was stagnating on both fronts, causing her career to stagnate as well.

Further, she reconfirmed for herself that she was an excellent rainmaker. As such, she met new people all the time. She might not love it, but she could do it and do it well. So, meeting new work colleagues wasn't as big a hurdle for her as her head was making it out to be. In time, she'd be comfortable with them as well, especially if she employed strategies aligned with her nature, such as setting up one-on-one conversations to meet coworkers and having time afterward to recharge.

Then we looked at her biggest objection, "starting all over." By casting her objection this way, Amy positioned the new job as if it were an offer to start at ground zero. Nothing could have been further from the truth. She'd be taking her reputation, her work product, and her clients with her. She'd also be making more money at a better firm. That is hardly "starting all over"—it's stepping up!

To ease her anxiety and allow her brain to process how it would go if she accepted the offer, we divvied up the stages of leaving her current firm and talked it through. Amy created a strategy for how she'd talk to her clients and give notice, how much time she'd take off between jobs, and what she might expect from her first week of work at the new firm.

She worried that clients wouldn't come with her, and even that concern didn't make sense when she examined it more closely. Amy was their lawyer—the only connection they had with her firm—and the new firm had more services to offer. Of course they would go with her. It was just another gambit by the brain to preserve the status quo.

Now motivated by a realistic look at her current circumstances, what she wanted, and what it would take to achieve it (not a fear of change), Amy accepted the offer at the new firm.

An aside, both Marjorie and Amy braced for recrimination when they gave their notice. Both were nervous about it. Marjorie faced none. Her coworkers congratulated her. They even threw her a little party on her last day. Amy, however, put up with anger and some childish behavior. One of her partners stopped speaking to her. My best guess is this was because Marjorie went in-house with a client and Amy took her clients with her when she left. Firms are usually more neutral about losing lawyers than clients. But Amy's colleagues should have at least been professional, if not wishing her luck.

The important thing here is that both Amy and Marjorie thought through their exits before handing in their notices. They had strategies ready for dealing with any emotional dustups, and that gave them the courage to act on their new decisions and not retreat from them. Ultimately, Amy saw the poor behavior of her colleagues as validation that she'd made the right decision. When you make a decision that results in change—any change—it is important to anticipate that others might react badly and for you to have a plan for that.

For most people, the brain's first reaction to change is going to be retreat from the threat it perceives. However, you can take some of the uncertainty out of change and soothe your emotions by looking at it as a process and breaking it down into steps. With each step, you become surer of your way, and your brain becomes more comfortable with your choice. In time, you'll look back on that original discomfort with a sense of appreciation, as your accomplishments pile up in the rearview mirror and you keep moving forward. Making change is like a Fitbit for the brain. The steps get easier over time as your resistance to it decreases.

ELIMINATING LIMITING BELIEFS

Whether we're giving in to sunk cost fallacies or a general fear of change, so many of the things we tell ourselves to defend our doubling down on past decisions are nothing more than our own self-limiting beliefs—untrue axioms we've gotten from our families, our schooling, and our culture at large. Again, it is being aware of our particular limiting beliefs that allows us to catch them and bring them into our awareness, where we can dispel them and free ourselves to make a new decision.

Seth, a twenty-nine-year-old associate in a Philadelphia litigation practice, wasn't meeting expectations related to marketing, billable hours, and delegation. Because he was extremely well-liked and a good lawyer who showed promise, his firm hired me to coach him.

As we neared the end of our six-month contract, Seth had made marked improvement in every area we'd been told to work on. His boss was satisfied. I, too, thought things had gone well, as we'd been very successful.

Then, at our second-to-last session, Seth looked at me and sighed in a weary way well beyond his years. "If I had it to do all over again," he said, "I would just become a science teacher." I was taken aback. "Why would you think it's too late to do what you really want?" I asked. He looked at me. He didn't answer. Then he changed the subject. Since I wasn't his career coach (his firm hired me to work on specific deliverables), we returned to his agenda, putting the finishing touches on his action plan.

However, my question apparently stuck with Seth. At our very next session, he told me he'd decided to become a science teacher. Since our last conversation, he had been trying to think of a reason why it would be too late to change careers, but he couldn't. He had talked to his wife and made up his mind.

That's the funny thing about transformation. It can take years or just one question to create a moment of clarity and purpose. Seth thought about the changes he'd made in coaching—the increased billable hours, networking, and marketing—and realized that this would be the way forward if he stayed in the law. He would have to maintain these practices, year in and out. It was not for him.

At first, I worried that his firm, the one that hired me, would be disappointed, as it appeared I'd coached Seth right out of his job. But I realized, as did the managing partner, that Seth would never have been really happy there. Or in law. His situation could have dragged on for years, depriving the firm of finding what they wanted—an eager attorney to groom for partnership—and depriving Seth of the career he wanted. It was better for all that Seth stopped basing his decision on the self-limiting belief that it was "too late" to make a change and started making decisions based on present circumstances and information.

Over the next few years, Seth continued to work part-time at the firm while he returned to school to get his teaching certificate. He is now a full-time teacher, and happy at work. The firm hired an associate in Seth's place who is completely aligned with the work and is ambitious to succeed. It is a better fit for everyone.

BUT IT DOESN'T MAKE FINANCIAL SENSE

Perhaps the beliefs that limit us most and keep us clinging to past decisions are the ones we hold around money. Kristen's path had been a privileged one. Ivy League law school, law review, federal judicial clerkship. After graduating top of her class, she was now on the trajectory to make partner, defending class action lawsuits in a national law firm. From all outward appearances, Kristen was headed for big success in big law.

But she wasn't happy.

In her heart, Kristen felt called to nonprofit work. She'd even procured an offer with a legal-aid nonprofit that worked with children in need of special education services and their families. To her, it seemed like the perfect job, except she couldn't reconcile trading her $190,000 salary for a job that paid $90,000—especially considering the cost of law school, even though her parents paid for it, and she was debt-free.

Kristen's assessment revealed the highest score in altruism I'd ever seen—100 percent, the highest score possible. She cared deeply about helping people and about social justice, and she was sensitive, caring, and kind. So, it wasn't a shock that defense litigation was not panning out in terms of personal fulfillment for her. The only beneficiaries of Kristen's labor were big companies. Sometimes she even had to stick it to the little guy, which pained her. The work she did for them felt empty to her. Still, she kept bumping up against her belief that it made no financial sense to leave this higher-paying track.

As we peeled back the layers, Kristen's justifications began weakening, as self-limiting beliefs often do. Did she have massive student debt to pay off? No. Did she need her corporate salary to pay the mortgage? No. Her husband was also an attorney, but an engaged and enthusiastic one, who actively encouraged her to follow the path she wanted. He made more than enough money for their family, liked his work, and wanted the same for his wife, even if it meant a lower income. The cost of living in their area was relatively low compared with major cities as well.

The limiting belief that it made no financial sense to take the lower-paying job was off the table. Finances weren't a consideration here. Her law school education was expensive, that was true. But it was already paid for, so the money could not be recouped, placing it solidly in the column of sunk cost.

With her limiting belief dispelled, Kristen was running out of reasons to stick with a decision that wasn't serving her. She took the nonprofit job. As she rose through the ranks to become a supervising attorney, she made another decision based on her current circumstances and the future she envisioned for herself. She decided to get her master's in special education and fulfill her altruistic dreams.

You might be thinking, *How nice for Kristen to have her education paid for and a partner who can foot the other bills. I don't have anyone offering to cover my expenses, so finances do rule my decisions.*

I hear you. Most of us have nowhere near Kristen's advantages or resources. I certainly didn't when I stopped doubling down and made the decision to find a different area of law to practice. I had student loans and was my family's main breadwinner. It mattered how much a job paid. All that meant, however, was that finances needed to be factored into my decision—but they were not the only factor.

I'm guessing that if you take an honest look at your current situation, finances were not the sole determining factor in whether you took the job you have now. So, they should not be the sole determining factor keeping you there.

For those of us who are money challenged with debts to pay, finances are a feature in our career by design, but they do not constitute the whole design. You don't have to be rich to afford to change.

KNOWING WHEN TO RETHINK A DECISION

You've probably noticed that the automatic thought processes our brains employ to keep us doubling down are subtle, making them insidious. They can feel so usual, so socially acceptable, so rational that we don't even notice them. It takes practice to consistently identify sunk cost fallacy thinking, limiting beliefs, and a common aversion to change.

Luckily, the discomfort of being stuck in the wrong situation is not subtle. It shouts that it is time to rethink the decision that put you here. And if you dare double down, it keeps hurting until you do notice. So, while you're getting familiar with your brain's more understated mind games, you can look for these various discomforts to let you know it might be time for a new direction:

1. **Having persistent regrets about your career path**

    If you find yourself persistently daydreaming about a fork in the road you once faced and wishing you had taken a different path, or ruminating (as I did) about making a practical decision instead of going for something you really wanted, consider it a nudge telling you it is time to rethink the path you're on and make a different decision now.

2. **Resenting your job**

    Maybe you were lulled into your current position by a big fat paycheck. Maybe you were pushed by anxious parents who wanted you to have a job. Maybe you thought this was the area of law for you. But now that you're here, you find yourself resenting the work, your clients, everything. Pay attention. Is this the way you want to go through life? Resentment is a clear indication something needs to change.

3. **Justifying**

    The flip side of resentment is justifying. If you find yourself defending your choice to stay where you are (in your own head, as well as to other people), it's a signal you're no longer in the right place for you. Repeatedly saying "I have to because . . ." says you're out of alignment. It is time to reevaluate your last decision and realign with a new direction.

4. **Wishing for a do-over**

   If you're pining for a second chance and thinking, *If only I could do it all again*, you're probably ripe for a change. But framing your new decision as a "do-over" or "starting from scratch" isn't helpful. Your current job wasn't a mistake. It just doesn't fit anymore. Maybe it never did. That doesn't matter. How is it working for you now? And what might work better? That's where to focus your new inquiry and decision.

5. **Feeling restless**

   Restlessness often descends when a client is at the top of their game and still finds it lacking. They get a feeling there must be more to life than this. Whenever it strikes, restlessness is saying it is time to revisit your values and recalibrate your career.

6. **Feeling dread, sadness, or crying at the thought of going to work**

   If none of those other signals get you to stop doubling down, chances are you'll end up here—having negative emotional and physical reactions to the thought of going to work. Could there be any surer sign that you are in the wrong place and it is time for some new decisions?

7. **Being plagued by stress-related illnesses**

   If you are suffering from digestive problems, headaches, depression, anxiety, insomnia, and so on, it may be work-related. As I mentioned in the introduction to this book, the last phases of my life in litigation were accompanied by a host of stress-related health problems. My body was staging a protest to stress. If I wouldn't do something about my situation, my body was prepared to keep signaling until I did. I went to doctors, did physical therapy, and took medication. New things kept popping up, until I finally addressed the root cause. Within a short period after leaving litigation behind, my health improved. It was that simple. And hard.

What all these signals are trying to get you to look at is this: if your current job were a present opportunity, would you take it? If your answer is no, and yet you find yourself turning away from other opportunities, do some interrogation. Ask yourself why. Consider keeping a journal to note how often you experience these distress signals, under what circumstances, and what might they be pointing to that needs to change for you.

Entertaining change makes some people feel selfish. We think wanting change means we don't appreciate what we have. We think it seems indulgent to take on the risk that comes with change . . . or well-meaning parents or a spouse suggest as much. In truth, the selfish or indulgent thing is to double down on an old decision, to stay in the wrong place, to become angry and aggrieved, to not realize your full potential, and to not put your true passion and talents to use.

IT'S YOUR DECISION NOW

Even if your choice didn't lead where you hoped, there are no bad decisions really, just old ones that no longer fit your current circumstances or your future dreams. Your kindergarten career choice didn't detract from whatever choice you made next; likely it enriched it and your life. The job you are in now, whether you'd take it again or not, has taught you things you'll use to inform your next decision—both what you're looking for and what you're not.

Respect the choices you made in the past because you had your reasons to make them at the time. Mine them for data. But don't allow them to keep you stuck or even have an unreasonably heavy influence on your life moving forward. Your past decisions may have been good ones at first, but if you feel an itch, or get a signal, accept that they might not be working for you anymore.

When you choose to double down on an old decision, you're still making a choice. You're deciding to not evolve. Past decisions control your current life only if you let them. Give yourself the gift of permission. Permission to admit that something isn't working, permission to seek out new options. (If you can't give it to yourself, find someone who will give it to you—a friend, colleague, coach, mentor, or therapist.) Do whatever it takes to stop looking in a rearview mirror. The future lies before you, not behind you, so that's where your decisions must be focused.

LAW 3 IN BRIEF

- To open ourselves to opportunity requires we make new decisions. We must be aware of doubling down on past decisions that no longer serve us.
- Know the difference between an expenditure and an investment when it comes to decision-making.
- Put the past in the past. When making decisions, your only considerations should be your current situation and your future plans.
- Be aware that our brains are wired to avoid change. Our biology employs automatic thought processes—sunk cost fallacy thinking, limiting beliefs, and general aversion to change—to encourage us to double down on old decisions and forgo considering new opportunities.
- Know the signals for when it is time to rethink a decision. When you experience one, journal about it to understand what it is telling you.
- Take responsibility for your decisions. Practice being future focused in your decision-making.

Law 4

Curate Your Career

> *"They always say time changes things, but you actually have to change them yourself."*
>
> —*Andy Warhol*

Successful collections have curators—someone charged with their care and superintendence. Someone with an overarching vision for them. Guided by that vision, curators build their collections—carefully selecting each piece for the value it adds. They strategically choose where they will exhibit and see to every detail of the show—organizing, arranging, and highlighting each piece so viewers experience the collection in a way that emphasizes its quality, underlines its meaning, and makes its value obvious.

Without a curator, a collection can lack cohesion. Because there is no one tending to the vision, pieces get added by chance, without thought or strategy. With no one to oversee its presentation, it can appear haphazard, its treasures lost in the randomness.

Viewers aren't sure what they're looking at, what to think of it, or how it all adds up.

The best curators never regard their collections as finished or static. They continually work to deepen its worth and relevance, further its vision, and add to its appeal.

YOUR CAREER IS YOUR COLLECTION

When we hear the word *collection*, we maybe think art, fashion, or rare books. But your career is a kind of collection, too. It consists of all the experiences that have brought you to this point—your education, internships, clerkships, work, memberships, networks, awards, accomplishments, and so on. Like all collections, if you are to achieve your vision for it, it must be strategically and continuously added to, thoughtfully managed, and always shown in the best light. So, you must become its curator.

Too many of us lawyers have episodic and reactive careers. Our only overarching vision is to "get ahead." Because we don't define what that looks like for us, we hop from one job to the next without a plan behind our moves. Or we stay in one place with our nose to the grindstone, hoping someone will notice and promote us. But to what position and to what end? This is the opposite of curating.

When he was young, Chris had a vision. He'd always wanted to be a lawyer. Always. He could not remember a time when it wasn't his ideal career. To that end, he made sure to distinguish himself in high school and college. This led to his attending an Ivy League law school. Which then led to an internship with the U.S. Department of Justice and a clerkship with a Superior Court judge. Step by strategic step, he checked all the boxes to land a high-powered, prestigious position as a lawyer. Sure enough, right out of law school, Chris was offered a job as an associate at an Am Law 100 firm, one of the biggest in the country, in its New York office.

His original vision achieved, like so many of us, Chris stopped doing things to develop and promote himself and started doing as he was told, which meant meeting billable hour targets. Now eight years into that dream job, his career was going nowhere. His solution to his dissatisfaction was to look for another job (a common knee-jerk reaction to being unfulfilled at work). What he found was other firms weren't jumping to hire him. Like with every other aspect in life, the problem wasn't his job, per se; it was him. The laurels that had landed him his current position had withered and eight years of doing a good job wasn't enough to get something better.

Though he worked for a big, well-respected national firm, Chris was an associate to a partner who was a litigation generalist. So, while Chris had handled a good number of disputes, he had no particular expertise in any one specialty to offer another firm. And because he'd always worked primarily for one partner, he hadn't built his own book of business or had the opportunity to impress other partners. This wouldn't have mattered so much if he'd been three to five years in when he began his job search. But at eight years, firms understand that partnership is on the horizon, and so they look for a portable book or the demonstrated potential to have one in lateral hires.

ONLY YOU CAN CURATE YOUR CAREER

Right out of law school, Chris had been a star and in demand. Now he couldn't get an offer. He was even finding it difficult to market himself because he lacked identity as a lawyer. When people asked about his work, he didn't have a ready answer, he told me in a session.

In college and in law school, the steps to success are articulated. Get good grades, join clubs, go out for sports, engage in meaningful extracurricular activities, write for a law review, get a prestigious internship, clerk for a judge, and that will lead to a great job.

Once you are on the job, however, there is no guidance counselor or road map for how to progress or stay viable and relevant. No one tells us how to manage a caseload or deal with clients. No one shows us how to build our own book or network. We toil away under the false notion that if we work hard and do a good job, our careers will take care of themselves. They don't.

Chris made this classic mistake. He trusted the firm he joined to make sure he was progressing; to give him interesting, career-building cases; to identify what he needed to make partner. Chris trusted the firm so much that he focused all his efforts on doing a good job for them and assumed they'd reward him when the time was right. They didn't. (Even if they had, they would have been handing Chris the career of their choosing, not his.)

Again, like so many of us, Chris hadn't understood the agreement he unwittingly made when he took this job. In return for billing hours, he'd get a salary and benefits. That is it. Keeping to that agreement, the firm fed him a steady diet of lowly tasks on big cases—nothing that significantly added to his expertise or stature, increased his skill set, or even let him show his talents. His yearly reviews were glowing because he was a hard worker and racked up tremendous hours. But no one was talking about his future or a path to partnership—and he didn't ask either. In time, lawyers in his cohort began leaving the firm to take jobs in-house or at firms where they would have more opportunity. With no offers, Chris had no choice but to stay on.

Chris's classic mistake put him in a classic bind. He'd become an amazing advocate for everyone but himself. Eight years in and he was still an associate for a generalist and all evidence pointed to years of more of the same.

Chris knew things needed to change, but now he was coming around to understanding that he was the one who needed to change them. Instead of putting his effort into finding a new job, he needed to work on building a career—one he could be excited about. His focus now would be on securing the skills, profile, and network needed to both create and seize opportunities that would move him closer to his vision. Put succinctly, Chris would become the curator of his career.

Chris's assessment told us that his primary values were recognition, leadership, security, power, and influence. He needed acknowledgement and to be well known. He mostly wanted a career where he'd have impact, authority, and recognition. Being a "generalist" wasn't going to achieve that. He'd need to find a niche, an area of law where he could stand out.

Meeting your vision for your career, especially in a profession like the law, demands you to always be a few moves down the chessboard—looking out for what's next. You must think and advocate for yourself. You must continuously build your skills, reputation, and network. No one else is going to do it.

ELEVATE YOUR CURRENT SITUATION

Your current position is a piece in your collection. It is up to you to polish and develop it as best you can, to find opportunities in it that advance your vision for your career overall. Squeeze out whatever value you can. Where might you build skills? Increase your network? Get noticed? As the curator of your career, you make the job work for you.

Though Chris continued at the same firm, his attitude toward his job changed. He no longer waited for opportunity to come to him. He asked to loan himself out to different partners within the firm—diversifying his portfolio and broadening his visibility. He asked for specific assignments instead of only taking what his boss put on his desk—building his skill set and, arguably most important, showing himself that he could break out of the box the firm had planted him in. He took on a pro bono case to further build skills.

CLARIFY YOUR CURRENT STATUS

Chris also took the initiative to call a meeting with his boss to clarify his status with the firm and explore what a future there might hold for him. A common misconception among associates is that our supervisors are aware of our status—how we feel about our job, what's working for us, what isn't, and what we see for our future. We assume they know we want to make partner, too. We just assume all that because they work with us every day and they know us. That is a fallacy.

Unless you ask outright, you can't know what they think about you or your career or even if they think about you and your career. Unless you tell them directly what you want from your job and from them, you can't expect them to deliver it. Setting clear standards, terms, and expectations for how you work is part of curating your career. For Chris—and for you—at the very least, such a meeting provides the data needed to know if a future at your current firm is the future you want.

Before you rush into such a meeting, however, you must prepare. Figure out ahead of time both the information you want to express and how you can convey it in the most advantageous way for you. I often recommend clients read *Crucial Conversations: Tools for Talking When the Stakes Are High*, by Kerry Patterson, Joseph Grenny, Ron McMillan, Al Switzler, and Emily Gregory, to learn a few smart tactics for difficult conversations before making an appointment with their boss. Keep in mind that simply having a conversation about your future prospects is hardly high stakes, so don't make it scarier by elevating its significance. I also give clients the following prep strategies and tips to review for this particular conversation:

- Since you are the one initiating this meeting, have an agenda and a strategy for it. This doesn't need to be a formal, typewritten thing. But you do need to think through and get clear on the topics you wish to broach. Bring notes to the meeting if it helps, and be prepared to take notes as you gain information.

- Set the baseline for the conversation. Present your current situation. Let your boss know where you started with the organization, what you have done for them, what you are doing now, and how you feel about it, pros and cons. Again, don't assume your boss knows this. Always maintain a neutral, pleasant tone. Entitlement isn't appealing, but ambition can be.
- Give your boss room to respond to what you've said. Note if they seem surprised by the information. Or if they seem to be aware of your work and you. Note if they react defensively or if they're open to your point of view. All reactions provide good data for your decisions moving forward.
- Let them know of the future, if any, you'd like to have with the organization. What you want and need—more money, more variety, a promotion, a path to partnership. No ultimatums, though. Get clear on this in advance by thinking it through with these questions:
  o Why does your situation matter to your boss? What's in it for them? For the organization? Don't make it about you (even though it really is about you). Frame what you want as advantageous for them.
  o What exactly do you want to ask for? And what have you done to earn it? Be prepared to advocate for your accomplishments and hard work.
  o What will their objections be? When you're prepared for objections, you can answer them calmly and rationally. That is where your training to think like a lawyer is invaluable. You can see both sides of most situations if you try. Also, there is no benefit to arguing. Quite the opposite. By thinking through objections and having a counter ready, you can turn them to your advantage.

- o If they offer a plan for your future, listen to what they have
  to say. Take notes. But do not get pulled into their vision—
  remember, this is your collection. You are the curator here.
- Practice your approach. Have the full conversation with yourself in the mirror. Get comfortable taking the lead.
- Pick the time for this meeting carefully. Choose a time when
  you think your boss will be most receptive. This is key to your
  conversation's success. (Think about what happens when
  someone picks the wrong time with you.)
- Prepare for "yes." Know what you'll say—and what you won't
  say—if your boss says yes to everything you ask for.
- Prepare for "no." Be ready to ask what needs to improve for no
  to become yes. Press for specifics and an agreement, so when
  you've made those changes, you can go back and refer to the
  criteria discussed and already agreed upon.

When Chris finally sat down with his boss, he learned that this
person he'd served for eight years didn't really know him at all. His
boss had no idea what Chris's ambitions were or that he wanted more
responsibility. He certainly didn't recognize that Chris was languishing. However, his boss was attentive and listened to what Chris had
to say. The meeting ended with his boss promising to work with him
to grow his skills and help him progress at the firm.

But in the months ahead, his boss did none of those things.
However, Chris, now fully in curator mode, was proactive. He followed up with his boss, reminded him of their agreements, and
continued to ask for what he wanted. Again, his boss promised all
the right things and then buried Chris in work that was beneath his
skill level.

While somewhat depressing, this lack of any meaningful change
in his circumstances gave Chris all the data he needed to know there
was no future for him at this firm. Thus, Chris felt free to add value

to his "collection" where he could in his current job and prepare himself to make a move.

Note, it could have gone the other way for Chris. I've seen it happen. In other firms, with a different boss, Chris's initiative may have been rewarded. He might have been given new work, been invited to join a committee, had a mentor assigned. Some firms show associates the road to partnership and others keep the map to themselves. The important thing is not to wait on anyone else to determine your career. You choose your direction. You ask for what you want and need.

The practice of asking alone builds your confidence as a curator. You learn to stick up for yourself. You don't allow yourself to get taken advantage of. You also find out one way or another the next steps needed to add value to your collection. By elevating your current situation, you better position yourself to take full advantage of all prospects that come your way.

UPGRADE YOUR OFFERINGS

As a good curator of your career, you also, obviously, want to look beyond your current circumstances. You want to be continually upgrading what you have to offer, continually investing in what will make you the professional you want to be.

For some of us that means investing in more education to add skill sets, specific knowledge, or credentials. Luckily, accessing quality education on most any subject has never been easier. These days, there's a world of choice when it comes to experts wanting to teach and platforms on which you can learn. In addition to traditional, in-person seminars, workshops, and classes, many organizations and individuals offer online courses. Whatever it is you need to upgrade what you offer, type it into a search engine and find the right source to teach it to you.

Another area that improves our value and requires ongoing investment is staying on top of industry trends. You must be up to date with what's going on in the world and in your industry to be able to provide clients and firms the best advice. To get started, get (and stay) involved in pertinent industry groups in person and on social media, subscribe to trade magazines and newsletters, and set up news alerts for industry stories.

Many overlook this very easy upgrade—their appearance. First impressions are formed in seconds and are based largely on nonverbal factors such as how you look. As the curator of your collection, how you show yourself to the world is a big part of your job. You want to dress and groom yourself for the role you want. If you are wearing the same hairstyle you wore in law school, consider an update. If you don't know how to put together a professional look, find someone who can help you. Many department stores have personal stylists. Take advantage of their expertise. Whether fair or not, you are judged on your appearance—we all are. It's a simple upgrade and well worth the effort. When you look good, you feel confident as well.

As you invest in new knowledge and new skills, remember to add them to your résumé. Should you apply for a new job or respond to an offer, always customize and polish your résumé for that specific position. Use the posting as a recipe and include key words as ingredients. If you plan to apply for jobs online, consider hiring a certified résumé writer. They can optimize your résumé to survive online screening. Keep a running list of your accomplishments at work, too. Always be ready to discuss and describe them.

Growing your value takes regular and continual investment in what you offer—the whole package.

PROMOTE YOURSELF. MANAGE YOUR PROFILE.

Your network is your net worth—it's a cliché because it's true. When Chris first came to me for coaching, he didn't have much of a network because he'd spent the last eight years hunched over a desk cranking out work product. He ate lunch at his desk by himself every day and went straight home after a long day at work. He was not involved in any extracurricular activities or a member of any organization except his church, which he did not regularly attend.

Do not let this happen to you. If it has already happened, don't worry. You know people. You went to college and law school. You've had a job, interned, and met a variety of people. You can begin to build your network from there. This is what Chris had to do.

Whatever shape your current network is in and wherever you are starting from, the following will give you some ideas of where to look next and where you might be missing opportunities to connect. With your vision always top of mind, look for people with whom you can have a mutually beneficial relationship, as well as groups and activities that will add value to your career and heighten your profile.

- Contact old friends and associates. Bring them into your current world. Set up coffees, lunches, or drinks to catch up. Listen to them for ways you can be helpful in their work. Build trusting relationships of mutual benefit. Don't forget to add them as connections on social media.
- Identify and attend networking groups. Select them based on their likelihood to bring you into contact with career prospects or referral sources.
- Volunteer or join the board of a nonprofit you believe in. This will introduce you into circles beyond the law, add value on your résumé, and give other leaders in your community (potential clients) a way to come to know and trust you.
- Position yourself as a thought leader in your area of expertise. Write articles for trade publications. Guest blog. Get booked on podcasts and radio shows. It's a great way to get noticed. Printed words on a page with a byline or being introduced

as someone worth listening to is powerful when it comes to upping your profile.

- Speak in public. There's always demand for speakers at events. Keynoting or serving on a panel establishes you as an authority in front of people who are interested in your area of expertise. If your speaking skills are rusty or you need to overcome your fear of speaking in public, consider joining Toastmasters, an international organization with local chapters everywhere. Their sole mission is helping speakers improve and overcome any fears.

- Update your LinkedIn profile. Be sure to add your volunteer activities, speaking engagements, and articles. Use LinkedIn to ask for recommendations and endorsements to further build your reputation. Look for new connections that can advance your interests. Join groups. Invest time learning to use LinkedIn. It's a terrific tool for professional networking and raising your profile.

- Use social media to keep your network informed of your speaking events, promote your work, and continually build connections. Make sure your posts provide value and are not merely self-promotion.

- Work your new connections, and find out what their concerns are—maybe you can help them. Ask who they are affiliated with—if their affiliations are of interest, ask for introductions.

- Ask for help. This is an often overlooked way to build trust because asking for help makes you vulnerable. As an attorney, you regard yourself as someone who provides help, not someone who needs it. Asking for help is not weak; it's smart. It is the most direct route to the information you need and builds instant connection. Just think of how you feel about professionals you've helped.

To get the most from your growing network, keep track of your interactions with a customer relationship management (CRM) program, a spreadsheet, or something of your own design. Note how you met each person, where they work, and what you talked about. To keep your network active and working for you, create a system for following up and periodically touching base.

MENTORS, SPONSORS, AND CHAMPIONS

Nothing can add value to your career and move you toward your vision faster than having the support of mentors, sponsors, and champions—people who have been there and can show you the ropes. You want these people in your professional corner.

Mentors are identified and selected by you, the mentee. They excel at something you want to master and are willing to help you master it—such as how to navigate firm politics, get choice assignments, handle performance reviews, or deal with difficult clients. You might find them inside your organization or outside of it.

When I was a new lawyer at the School District of Philadelphia, I needed to get better at politics, government, and public perception. I looked around for who in the district stood out in those areas. To my surprise, the biggest standout was younger than I was. She was the director of the Charter Schools Office and not a lawyer, but I asked for her help just the same. She graciously mentored me through those tricky areas. Thanks to her, I didn't fall flat on my face in public.

To find the right mentor for you, think about which area in your career could use a fresh perspective from a more seasoned person. See who's a star in that arena and, like me, just ask. You might begin by stating what you admire about them and then move into the kind of help you are seeking. For instance, you might say, "I've noticed you are a terrific rainmaker. That's something I'm working on right now. I could really use some guidance. Would you consider meeting with me from time to time for some mentoring?" Then be sure to set a time to meet.

Sponsors are another rung above mentors because they will look for opportunities to increase your network, ask you to events, and make introductions. That is how you know a sponsor relationship is forming because, unlike mentors, sponsors are not selected. You earn them. They may start out as mentors and blossom into sponsors by being continually wowed—by you, at work or through business activities. Their value is that they've observed you professionally over time and, on their own, feel you are worth sponsoring. Whenever they can help you advance, they're willing to step up and speak on your behalf. If you are seeking a promotion or choice assignment, you can turn to your sponsor and ask them to sing your praises to the powers that be or support your endeavor.

Sponsors can grow into champions—a sponsor on steroids who will use their political capital to help you. They don't necessarily need to be asked. They pick up the phone proactively and tell someone why they ought to nominate, hire, and appoint you to a coveted position, or give you a career-making case. Like sponsors, champions are grown, not picked. They become invaluable in myriad ways to your success and happiness.

Part of curating your career is developing these relationships. You tend to them and help them mature by offering to help those who show potential for these roles when needed. You invite and keep such relationships by being impeccable with your word and being so reliable that someone is willing to stake their reputation and professional relationships on you.

WORTHWHILE COLLECTIONS TAKE COMMITMENT AND STRATEGY

To have a career by design, you must be vigilant about curating it. Fine collections don't come together quickly. They build, often slowly and without immediate reward.

Chris's career reset did not occur overnight, but it didn't take forever either. While still languishing at his firm, Chris took a lot of the small steps we've discussed in this chapter. He grew active in his church, joined a board, gave speeches, and adhered to a cycle of reaching out, consistently connecting with the new people in his network.

It's important to note that while nothing changed in his current job, Chris built his credibility through speaking and writing, and kept networking top of mind in all interactions. As he so succinctly put it, "Every week, I do stuff." Whether Chris was researching industries, guest blogging for a legal site, addressing the local Rotary club, or networking on the golf course, he was actively and consistently pursuing his vision.

There were, of course, times when Chris got frustrated and wished things were moving faster. He wondered out loud if this was going to work. He was eager to feel like he mattered. He wanted to be on a partner track. He wanted to be working on cases where he was the lead, where he felt he was making a difference directly, rather than behind the scenes.

But he kept working away at upping his value and his profile. One day, after a long dry spell, he received two good offers from decent firms. Both were for positions slightly better than his current one; both offered a higher salary.

Though he was flattered and anxious for change, he turned both offers down. Chris was no longer simply looking for a job. After evaluating the offers through the lens of a career curator, he realized the work itself was similar to what he was doing at his current firm. General litigation practice. Neither would add anything to his collection. Neither would move him closer to his vision. So, Chris chose to stay where he was and continue with his "doing stuff."

Not long after, Chris received an offer from a boutique law firm doing blockchain law (an area that didn't even exist when I was a lawyer). This was exactly what he'd been seeking—a role where he could become an industry expert in a growth field with a specialized niche practice. Chris accepted their offer.

At this new firm, he, of course, did the work he was assigned. He also used his new position to hone his skills in this specialty, expand his network, build his profile in blockchain law, and build his client book. He didn't eat lunch at his desk.

After only a year, he had two job offers from major firms in his new specialty. He wasn't even looking for a job. Now a known and respected blockchain specialist with a growing book of business, he was being recruited and could choose where he would take his practice.

He joined a major law firm, and this time, he knew exactly what he wanted from the firm and how to make partner. Note, it wasn't entirely the size of Chris's book of business that won over new firms. It was also his ability to demonstrate his marketing mindset. He could articulate his marketing plan, identify ideal clients, and demonstrate his networking and marketing activities. All one had to do was Google him to see how active and engaged he was now.

Today, Chris is a forever curator. Once he realized it was his job to create and curate his career, he took that power and built a career that continues to grow in value and meaning for him.

As a person in business for myself, I continue to curate my career. Each year, I add at least one new piece of value to my offerings. I take courses, earn certifications, and make it a point to meet experts who can increase my professional knowledge. I see it as an important part of my job to remain on the hunt for new solutions and strategies to help my clients and build my business.

Now it's your turn to become the curator of your career—to take charge rather than relying on others, to decide for yourself what your future will be, to always be conscious of where you want to head, and adding to your value to make sure you get there.

LAW 4 IN BRIEF

- If you want a career of value, you must tend to it. No one else is going to.
- Commit to becoming the curator of your career. This means measuring your choices and actions by the value they add to attaining your vision.
- Take inventory of your current career assets—education, experience, expertise, network, current position. Build from where you are. Find opportunities in your current circumstance that move you closer to your goal.
- Increase your value by continually upgrading what you offer. Think about the skills, experience, or certifications your vision requires. Then go get them.
- Increase your profile by continuously cultivating your network.
- Look for mentors, sponsors, and champions to support your career.
- Stick to it. Curating your career is an everyday activity. Understand that your efforts are cumulative.

Law 5

Mind Your Mindset

> *"Once you replace negative thoughts with positive ones, you'll start having positive results."*
>
> —*Willie Nelson*

Skeptics like to say, "I'll believe it when I see it." But if you are wishing for success, believing has to come first. Only when you believe in your ability to cause change will you begin to appreciate the possibilities present in your life. Right now.

What we believe drives what we do. What we do creates our destiny. If the goal is to move our careers out of default mode and into design mode, we need to move our thinking out of default mode, too. We need to train ourselves to check in with said thinking before we act and make sure that what we think or believe is (1) true and (2) advancing us toward the life we want.

Thus, Law 5: Mind Your Mindset.

In her best-selling book *Mindset: The New Psychology of Success— How We Can Learn to Fulfill Our Potential,* Carol Dweck, researcher and professor of psychology at Stanford University, writes about the difference between having a "fixed" versus a "growth" mindset. Of those two mindsets, she writes, "The view you adopt for yourself profoundly affects your life. It can determine whether you become the person you want to be and whether you accomplish the things you value."

With the right mindset, you can change just about anything in your life. We are way more powerful than we realize. The problem is we don't always make the connection between our mindset and our ability to perceive opportunities or anticipate and overcome obstacles.

WHAT MAKES A MINDSET

Our mindset or thought patterns are created from information accumulated over a lifetime. This information influences our current decisions and guides our actions. Some of that information comes from what we learn in childhood from our parents and other authority figures: "education is the key to success." Some we gain from our own experience: "homemade cookies are the best." And some we absorb from our culture: "you should always tip your server."

The bits of information we use most often can become strongly held beliefs. These beliefs stake out territory in our brains, gather prominence in our thought processes, and join other such robust views to form our mindset—a general rule book about the world that we keep in our heads and through which we filter everything.

When faced with a decision, our mind automatically goes to that rule book and pulls up what it thinks is the most pertinent information we have stored. Then we act on those thoughts without challenge. By default. Some of these notions get used so often and so dependably that our minds come to regard them as facts, when in reality, they are little more than opinions that have become our default responses.

To be sure, this automatic information-at-the-ready saves time and brain power as you steer through everyday events. But when you allow your brain to take this reflexive route for larger, more complex decisions (such as significant career changes), the result is you sell yourself—and what's possible for you—short. You may even sell yourself out.

When a decision is important, it's at least worth asking yourself about the beliefs, preferences, and attitudes that went into making it. They might be on point for the situation. Or they might be outdated, leading you in the wrong direction this time, or worse, keeping you stuck in a negative pattern of behavior.

Consider that many of your go-to attitudes may have been right when first introduced to your brain. They may even have served you well for years. But as you work to change and advance in your life and career, it only makes sense that some of them will need to change and advance along with you. That means making a practice of bringing awareness to your thought patterns, challenging those thoughts, and updating where necessary. It means unfixing your mindset and making room for more dynamic thinking.

NO CHALLENGE, NO CHANGE: UNFIXING YOUR MINDSET

Many lawyers struggle with a fixed mindset when it comes to their careers. This is not surprising, really. From our first days in law school, we are taught "the way it's going to be"—long hours, no personal life, the hierarchal nature of the profession, and so on. Once we begin practice and those expectations are met, our experience confirms what we were told, and so naturally, we operate from that mindset.

But that fixed mindset presumes that nothing changes in this world or in the practice of law. That situations don't evolve. That you don't evolve. That character, intellect, and creative aptitude are static. That the limits have been set. Such a mindset—thinking the particulars of your career are preordained—prevents you from exploring, inquiring, investigating, and designing and pursuing the career of your dreams.

Take Charlie, for example. For nearly ten years, his Philadelphia practice focused on criminal law exclusively—and so of course, he thought of himself as a criminal attorney. Then a handful of appellate cases came his way. To his surprise, he really liked the work. In fact, he greatly preferred appellate law to criminal law. And he was good at it. As he was finishing up his last appellate case, he found himself wishing another would come across his desk—or better yet, that he could switch his entire practice to appellate law.

Almost as soon as he entertained that dream, however, his mindset shut it down. His set of beliefs about how things worked in the legal profession told him that he was too inexperienced to market himself as an appellate attorney. In our first coaching session, Charlie shared his dilemma: "I've only ever handled six appellate cases, so I can't really promote myself as an appellate lawyer. But if I can't attract more appellate cases, how can I ever get the experience to switch my practice?"

"Six cases!" I said right back. "I considered myself an appellate attorney after completing my first oral argument before the Pennsylvania Commonwealth Court."

Obviously, I had a completely different mindset than Charlie in this matter—which proved that both our beliefs were subjective, not factual. I asked him why a decade in criminal practice and six appellate cases under his belt weren't enough experience to solicit more appellate work. Where was that rule? Who said so? How many cases would qualify him to be an appellate attorney? Ten? Twenty?

With just that little bit of challenge, Charlie's mindset shifted. He understood immediately that his standard for what constituted "an appellate attorney" was based on nothing more than an arbitrary "belief" he'd picked up along the way and set in his mind as truth. The real truth was there was no magic number that would make him a bona fide appellate attorney.

Right then and there, Charlie's mindset evolved and updated its data to meet the reality of his new circumstance. All his "reasons" why he couldn't become an appellate attorney—to do what he wanted in his life—fell apart under scrutiny. By the end of our conversation, he'd given himself permission to call himself an appellate attorney. The next day, he began moving his practice in that direction. (By the way, he eventually sold his appellate practice for a healthy seven figures and happily embraced a new family-centered phase of life.)

When you find yourself thinking, *I couldn't possibly*, even though you want to desperately, take it as an invitation to challenge your mindset around that issue or circumstance. It is true that you can't? Why? What authority says so? What would happen if you did? Maybe most important, where will you remain if you don't?

Remember, no challenge, no change.

THE FOREST FOR THE TREES

Eve, a government lawyer, dreamed of making law school instruction more engaging for students. Using a discipline known as instructional design, she created courses and materials that met students' needs and made learning more experiential. After scoring a part-time job in instructional design, she wanted to make it her career. For months, she'd been pursuing full-time positions in the field with no success.

When she shared her résumé and cover letters with me, the reason for her failed job search was glaringly apparent. She'd presented herself to prospective employers as a career changer, someone who "was in government law, now" but wanted "to pivot to a career in instructional design" using "transferable skills." I'm sure most employers never read past the word *pivot*. After all, they were looking to hire someone who could do the job already, not someone moving toward it, someone they would have to train.

As Eve and I talked, I came to understand that from her perspective, leaving government service completely and taking a full-time job at a law school was a full-blown career transition. That's the way her mind was framing it. So that's the story she put forward in her cover letters and résumé.

"This is not a pivot or a transferable skill situation," I pointed out. "You're already doing the work you're seeking. You have the skills. The only real change will be the number of hours you'll spend doing instructional design each week."

I could see Eve's mind making the shift. She realized that to her, "part-time" equaled "hobby," "trying it out," or "not real." This caused her to discount the very real, on-the-job experience she already had, which was preventing her from seeing what an attractive candidate she was to potential employers. The work she sought was the work she was currently and successfully doing. After thinking it through, she decided it would be more accurate to present herself as "a currently employed instructional designer looking for a new role." She also needed to own that herself.

With that one tweak to her mindset, Eve was able to repackage herself in a way that represented her true value proposition. She rewrote her résumé and cover letters to reflect the reality of her skill set and experience. Within a few months, she was working full-time doing instructional design for a law school.

MINDSET CREEP

Charlie and Eve were both able to shift their mindsets quickly by challenging an obvious block in their thinking in one circumstance.

But sometimes obstructive mindsets are such a part of us, so ingrained in how we see the world and ourselves, that it takes deeper probing and a more sustained effort to update or change them.

Jenn, a fifth-year litigation associate in a global law firm, wanted to make partner. Her performance evaluations showed she was a good lawyer—smart, dependable, a hard worker, and well-liked by colleagues and clients. What she was lacking was confidence and independence. She rarely offered solutions in meetings and was timid about making decisions on her own. If she wanted to progress at the firm, she knew she had to step outside her comfort zone.

As much as she wanted to be bolder and more self-directed, she just couldn't put herself out there no matter how hard she tried. The risk felt too great on so many levels.

After talking with Jenn, it was apparent that what was limiting her opportunities wasn't one or two misguided thoughts about the practice of law. It was a mindset full of long-held, deep-seated beliefs about herself. For instance, Jenn worried that she wasn't as smart as everyone seemed to think and that someday people were going to realize that and call her on it (a.k.a., imposter syndrome). She believed one wrong move, one bad decision could get her fired—which kept her from making decisions on her own and taking credit for her ideas. Jenn also took it upon herself to keep everyone at the firm happy—she wanted no confrontation. Which turned her into the consummate people pleaser, taking time and energy away from substantive work that would position her for partnership.

I rarely work with an attorney who doesn't bring at least a smidge of these same issues into their work. Especially imposter mindset. And it's not exclusive to women. This self-defeating belief transcends pedigree, status, and privilege. Ivy League grads in high-powered jobs, million-dollar verdict winners, and partners in law firms all contend with the nagging thought that one day the secret of their incompetence will come out.

However, for Jenn, this and the rest of her paralyzing mindset were taken to the extreme. Looked at as a whole, her problematic behaviors seemed to stem from one underlying root belief—that if she wasn't perfect, if she made a mistake, if people didn't like her, she'd face rejection. In her mind, rejection was unendurable.

Such a pervasive, negative notion was likely planted in early life. So, over the years, she'd constructed a mindset to ensure she avoided rejection at all costs. Those costs, however, turned out to be quite high—as in being overlooked, never getting credit, and being seen as less than she really was.

Then law school—where saying no is discouraged and perfectionism is set out as a professional standard—reinforced and further cemented her mindset. (By the way, saying yes to everything and wedding yourself to perfection are not advisable for success in the law or in life. These behaviors may win you a few kudos early in your career, but after a while, they impede achievement because they stunt thought and performance.) When you are invisible, you may not be criticized, but you also won't be promoted.

ALIGNING THE MINDSET TO THE MISSION

Intellectually, Jenn got all this. But in everyday practice, her thoughts and behaviors remained stuck in default. If she was going to change, she needed to replace her fear of rejection with an embrace of self-worth. Jenn needed to create new automatic thought processes that would result in new behaviors and change her career trajectory. She needed a mindset aligned with her current circumstances and with the truth of who she was now, what she was capable of, and what she wanted for herself.

Building a whole new mindset is like building a muscle. You don't expect to do one curl and see a bicep pop out. You must work at it diligently and consistently. You strengthen it from the inside until it shows on the outside.

Jenn decided to begin her mindset restructuring by joining a gym. Although this seems counterintuitive—working on your body to change your mind—it was exactly the right first step for Jenn.

Her whole life, Jenn's mindset had led her to put the needs of others first. At the office, this resulted in twelve-hour days at her desk working on whatever she'd been handed, never objecting to her workload, and spending more weekends than not on her couch catching up on work she'd promised to deliver by Monday. When she looked in the mirror now, she saw someone who'd put herself on the back burner for far too long. She felt sluggish, out of shape, and invisible. She wanted to take some time for herself, build muscle tone, have more energy, and feel better overall.

The mere act of joining the gym signaled to her brain that she was taking charge of her life. It made her invest real money in herself for the first time in a long time—strengthening her growing belief that she was worth investing in. It also made her commit time to a routine of self-care. For one hour a day, three days a week, she'd work solely on herself.

Three hours a week isn't that much when you think about it. Yet, many lawyers consistently deny themselves even that modicum of self-care. Through Jenn's consistency and progress with her workout routine, she not only learned but also experienced that she was good at self-directing—making decisions, taking action, achieving goals all on her own. With every free weight lifted and every new "personal best" attained on the treadmill, her mindset was evolving and shaping up as well.

"I love going to the gym," Jenn said after a few weeks. "I feel better physically. I also feel more accomplished."

In his book *The Power of Habit*, Charles Duhigg explains that once ingrained, a habit can set off a chain reaction of other behaviors. That's exactly what happened for Jenn. Investing in her physical well-being led to her valuing herself more and taking better care of herself in other ways. She started eating better, paying more attention to her clothes. She even took a risk on a new haircut, which people noticed and complimented her on. All of these things added mightily to her self-confidence and mindset of self-worth.

When you take a situation and change it through intentional actions, your power grows and your internal resources expand. With each passing day, Jenn could depend more and more on her improved thinking, and her behaviors followed to support her. When she was presented with a decision, her thought processes now made room for her to consider herself and what she wanted and needed. In time, this mindset made its way into the office and showed up as self-confidence.

Part of the way Jenn had coped at work with feelings of inadequacy and fear of rejection was by volunteering for lots of committee work, planning firm functions, and never saying no. She depended on her people pleasing to allay her fears of rejection. But here's the thing about people pleasing. It's never enough. When others realize they can dump on you, they never stop. If you can't say no, you will find yourself buried in a pile of yesses. You will be forever helping further someone else's agenda while yours languishes.

Despite the partners praising Jenn for her committee work, they made it clear at raise and bonus time that they didn't see her as adding enough value to the firm. In their defense, organizing inner-firm events isn't billable, nor is it directly tied to client acquisition. Unintentionally, Jenn had focused on building alliance through compliance as a good firm citizen, at the expense of advancing her skills and marketing her own practice. If she wanted to increase her profile and make partner, Jenn knew she needed to take on more advanced billable assignments and say no to committee work.

Saying no doesn't come naturally to most of us—it certainly didn't to Jenn. No takes practice. By its nature, it feels confrontational, something we all like to avoid. But you can't throw a stone in the lake without making ripples. No is going to be uncomfortable. The key is to be prepared for that discomfort and ready yourself to accept it.

Think of it this way: saying yes is going to be uncomfortable, too. Saying yes to an obligation you don't want will put you in a situation you don't want to be in. While insincerely saying yes may feel good in the moment, you know from experience the pain that follows. You know the slow, uncomfortable dread, along with a general irritation at yourself for being a people-pleasing pushover, only intensifies as the date of whatever you committed to this time marches closer on your calendar.

So, what any decision really comes down to is choosing which form of discomfort you'd rather have—one that puts you where you don't want to be or the one that takes you where you want to go.

No longer ruled by a fixed mindset, Jenn was finally able to see her committee work as a choice, and she chose to say no and let someone else take a turn.

Resigning from the committees continued to cause Jenn anxiety, of course. Her new mindset wasn't so strong that it completely kept her from fretting over what other people would think and whether the work would get done without her. But fear of rejection was no longer the primary driver. It was still in the car, but now in the passenger seat, and Jenn knew she could manage her feelings.

Her new thinking was that if other committee members felt she was letting them down, then (1) that would be confirmation of how valuable her contributions had been to the committee's work, and (2) the payoff for stepping aside and focusing on her career was worth momentary and fleeting feelings of rejection. With every decision and every action, Jenn's mindset was aligning with her goals.

One day while discussing strategy for a client call, her boss said, "You can take the call on your own if you want or I can be there with you. You decide." Jenn knew he was telling her he believed she could handle the call by herself. She thought about it for a second and realized she, too, felt she could handle it. And she did. That marked the beginning of Jenn, the proactive, decision-making, independent lawyer. From that moment on, she handled most things at work on her own.

At her next performance review, the partners praised her professional maturity, the increasing complexity of her work, and her decision-making. One partner said, "Jenn exhibits confidence rarely seen in young associates." What? Was he talking about the same woman who thought she was invisible and one bad decision away from being fired?

Jenn's mindset overhaul resulted in her receiving the highest bonus and raise possible. It makes sense that confident people make more money because they command it. More important, in her own mind, Jenn went from imposter to genuine impresser—abandoning both people pleasing and perfectionism. That's the product of minding your mindset and making sure you are working from a constructive set of beliefs. While Jenn's transformation wasn't as fast as Charlie's or Eve's, it only took about six months for her to make a noticeable impression upon the partners at her firm.

BUILDING A DYNAMIC MINDSET

It is up to us to bring awareness to our mindset and the natural outcomes that flow from it. We decide if we are going to allow our decisions and actions to be governed by ideas, beliefs, and attitudes that have been trolling around in our heads unexamined for years or if we're going to pay attention to the thoughts we use to determine our lives.

A dynamic career—one that is on the move in a positive way—requires a dynamic mindset, one that can entertain new thoughts and ways of seeing a situation. To keep your mindset vibrant, current, and working for you, make a habit of these four steps.

Step 1: Before you commit to any big decision or action, pause

Take a time-out and a deep breath. Bring awareness to the moment, to your decision or action, and to your thought process. Give your mind space to open to other possibilities.

Step 2: Once your mind is calm and open, review how you came to your decision or situation

What beliefs, attitudes, preferences, or personal perspective were used? Were you being motivated by fear or anxiety? Were you afraid someone would be angry with you if you did or didn't do something? Does your decision now feel off—even though you think you're right? Use your answers to identify any areas where your thought process may be out of touch with your goals and who you are today.

Step 3: Replace unproductive thoughts with more productive thoughts

You may have old recordings playing in your head, and it is up to you to delete them and create new ones. If your discernment tells you it's one belief or a simple perspective that needs alteration (like with Charlie or Eve), find a way to make the change. But if the issue is foundational to your mindset and showing up in several areas of your life, start slowly (like Jenn). Pick one area to create some momentum and build from there. Reinforce productive thoughts by anchoring them with a statement like, "When I say no to someone else, I say yes to me."

Step 4: In general, be proactive about developing a mindset more attuned with your vision

Here are a few exercises to get you started:

- Notice your self-talk. Write it down. Then read it back to yourself. Is what you are telling yourself helpful? Is it true for you today? For the situation? Or is it time for a reframe? And how often is it happening?
- Observe how you take a compliment. Step up and take credit when things go well. This helps maintain a positive mindset about your abilities because it establishes the connection between your efforts and good business results. Don't think to yourself and don't say out loud to the person who complimented you that "it was just luck" when you know it wasn't. Or that credit should go to someone else when it shouldn't.
- Seek constructive feedback and use it. We can't always see our patterns or test our points of view. Ask a trusted friend or colleague where they think your thinking may be off or keeping you stuck. Then consider the answers and make updates and changes where necessary.
- Create a "Me File" where you keep a list of all your skills, compliments, accomplishments, and achievements. Use it to preserve any praise you receive from clients, coworkers, and supervisors. Update this file as needed—so your mind is clear on what you are capable of and how valuable others find you.
- Create a mindset vision board. (Yes, I'm serious.) Find images that evoke what it looks like and feels like to have the mindset you want. Whatever it is: being confident, creative, innovative, a good leader, and so on. Look for words, phrases, and images that evoke that mindset. Keep that board where you can see it to keep your mindset top of mind, where it should be. In 2020, when the world shut down because of the pandemic, I made a vision board for the mindset I wanted to have: strength and resilience.

Your current life and career are an expression of your past decisions and actions, as determined by your mindset. If you want to have more control over the direction of your career and life from this moment forward, it's imperative that you take control of your thoughts.

Mastering your mindset is like getting the keys to a cage you've been locked in forever (albeit one of your own making). Careers by design are not achieved through default thinking. They come about through awareness, through minding your mindset, and keeping it primed and ready to take you in a new direction.

LAW 5 IN BRIEF

- Your mindset is a system of beliefs collected over a lifetime. Beliefs are not facts. They are just thoughts you've had for a long time. Some serve you well, some do not.
- Mindset plays a huge role in your decisions and actions—and thus, your destiny.
- For your career to evolve, your mindset must evolve as well. Examine your belief system to ensure it is aligned with your reality today. No challenge, no change.
- Sometimes all it takes is a quick look at your thought process. Are you holding a belief as if it were fact? Is it true? Does it serve you?
- Sometimes, if the belief that's keeping you stuck is deeply rooted, you need a mindset overhaul—requiring changes on the inside to effect changes on the outside.
- Curb your default thinking and bring awareness to your thought processes. Update as needed. Only you can mind your mindset.

Law 6

Hone Your Soft Skills

> *"I've learned that people will forget what you said, people will forget what you did, but people will never forget how you made them feel."*
>
> —*Maya Angelou*

I made a client cry once when I was a young lawyer. Obviously, not a proud moment for me. I wish it hadn't happened. But there it is, lodged inconveniently in my history and memory.

I was handling a big case. My client was a lawyer, too, and more seasoned than I. A judge had just been assigned to the case, and the client called to let me know her opinion of that judge, which was different from my firm's take on him. I should have welcomed that information. But being the insecure novice I was, I got extremely defensive. I cut my client off midsentence and told her the firm's stance on the judge in no uncertain terms. Taken aback by my bite, she stumbled over her words. Then she began to cry and hung up.

I was dumbfounded. As I contemplated what to do next, she called back to apologize. For me, that is the very worst part of the story. I should have been the one calling her to apologize—for not listening, for thinking my opinion was more important than hers, for not taking advantage of her experience, and for interrupting her (a client!) when she was speaking.

What I was missing in that early stage of my career, and what many attorneys fail to employ throughout their careers, were soft skills— such as empathy, patience, and simple courtesy. I was so busy proving my knowledge (a hard skill) that I was devoid of consideration toward my client (a soft skill). I was doing a great job on the case, but not on the client. And if you don't have a client, you don't have a case.

Earning your JD is evidence that you have the hard skills to be a lawyer. However, as you know, hard skills are not enough. As we attorneys progress in our careers, we are expected to manage client relationships, direct staff, and develop business. These activities require soft skills, and soft skills require emotional intelligence, also known as emotional quotient (EQ).

Thus, succeeding in this profession to the point of being able to call the shots in your own career means following Law 6: Hone Your Soft Skills.

YOUR EQ MATTERS AS MUCH AS YOUR IQ

Soft skills encompass all the relational skills we use to build any type of affiliation in business and life—empathy, communication, flexibility, critical thinking, and leadership, to name a few. Labeling these skills as "soft" may be a misnomer, though. They are the foundational bedrock of any successful career. They are tougher to measure than hard skills, to be sure, and even tougher to put into practice, especially if they've been drummed out of you by law school.

We spend so much time in law school learning to think like lawyers, we forget to think like human beings. We learn to become skeptics, a handy trait to have when investigating a case, but not so great when talking with a prospect. We build skills in fault-finding and finger-pointing, so we can then apply case law to identify culprits, affix blame, and find liability in what to anyone else would seem as simply a sorry situation. Most critical, we learn to keep our emotions from "clouding" our thinking.

All of this might work well for us when it comes to delivering a fact-based, winning argument in court. It's not so great for building trust and gaining influence with our teams, our clients, and people in general. In the world outside the courtroom, the facts are only part of the story. When navigating life and building a career, having hard skills without soft skills is a bit like having a skillet without fire.

Sure, we all know (and maybe even have worked for) attorneys who are mean, nasty, and devoid of soft skills but still make it to the top. Such situations are almost always created out of deference to the money generated by that person. Only in fairy tales are geese that lay golden eggs killed. In reality, they're promoted. While it will always be true that blind eyes to bad behavior do exist for those select few, it's also true that being thought of as a jerk by everyone you know is a pretty miserable way to go through life, no matter how much revenue you bring to your firm.

Soft skills allow us to cultivate the relationships that help us support and advance our careers—not to mention, give our work and lives meaning. They also make us better lawyers. While that client I made cry might have gotten me fired for my callousness (and I would have deserved it), the more important takeaway from that incident is that my defensiveness interfered with my ability to listen before offering counsel or advice. Failing to listen prevented me from making the best decision because I didn't get the client's input. And I failed to uphold the client's confidence both in our firm and in the law. Thus, this rudeness on my part could have had severe consequences when it came to strategy and securing a win.

For me to have been aware of my lack of soft skills and its consequences in that moment would have taken emotional intelligence on my part that I did not have. Daniel Goleman, in his groundbreaking book *Emotional Intelligence: Why It Can Matter More Than IQ*, defines EQ as having four domains: self-awareness, self-management, social awareness, and relationship management. Within those domains, he identifies twelve competencies: emotional self-awareness, emotional self-control, adaptability, achievement orientation, positive outlook, empathy, organizational awareness, influence, coach and mentor, conflict management, teamwork, and inspirational leadership. These are not elements law students think about much while hunched over a casebook in a study carrel.

Someone with a high EQ can walk into a business and have a meaningful exchange with anyone—from the janitor to the president. They are neither inhibited by nor intimidated by status—yours or theirs. They are able to listen, observe, and then identify and attend to the real issue at hand. How valuable would those attributes be to your law career?

EQ PAVES THE WAY FOR SOFT SKILLS

Jeff definitely didn't think about his EQ or the career benefits of employing soft skills. A midlevel associate, he was on the rise when clients and coworkers started complaining about his behavior, saying that he was easily irritated and took his frustration out on others. He'd been referred to me by a coach who no longer wanted to work with him. In getting me up to speed on Jeff, that coach succinctly described him as—and I quote—"an arrogant asshole."

At our first meeting, Jeff did not disappoint. He bristled at having been "sent for coaching" by his law firm. He argued that he was one of the hardest-working associates in the firm and had the most billable hours (both true). He informed me that any problems he was having with clients or coworkers were incidental in his view and not representative (not true). He then let me know that he doesn't come to work to make friends, but to provide for his family. His sense of entitlement was evident, as was his conviction that he did nothing wrong. He didn't believe anyone had a problem with him and, if one or two did, that's their problem.

Ah, but it was his problem. He was the one meeting with me, not his coworkers, not his clients. However, I didn't think Jeff was an "asshole." I saw in Jeff some of the same limitations that blind-sided me as a young lawyer. He layered his fear and insecurity with a veneer of certainty and haughtiness. It was a form of self-protec-tion. While it made him obnoxious to deal with, it didn't make him a bad person.

The first step in helping Jeff build some soft skills into his inter-actions with others was getting him to accept he had a problem and realize that if that problem was not taken care of, it would impede on his stated goal of "providing for his family." And that meant upping his EQ.

Easier said than done. Jeff was so focused on his own well-crafted identity and reasoning that he completely dismissed data about his reputation from his personality assessments—which found him to be highly skeptical of others, arrogant, curt, with low sociability and interpersonal sensitivity. It didn't matter to him that these were the same findings reported in his last performance review and in the complaints that sent him to coaching in the first place.

If he didn't like that data, I suggested he seek feedback from colleagues he admired and trusted. I suggested a 360-degree assess-ment, where a human resources person, coach, or consultant would conduct interviews to determine how he was to work with, for, and as a direct report to manage. Handling such an assessment through a professional not only makes it easier on the person being evaluated but also on the persons being surveyed. Thus, the results are likely to be more accurate.

But Jeff being Jeff, he wanted to approach his colleagues himself. He asked them what they thought of his management style and how they believed others in the workplace experienced him.

Remarkably, his colleagues didn't sugarcoat their answers. They told him exactly their impressions of him and backed up their statements with specific observations of his behavior in a variety of circumstances and with different people. To put it mildly, his colleagues' observations matched the findings of his assessment, his performance reviews, and the complaints against him. Faced with this evidence, Jeff could no longer deny his behavior was a problem—and with that he gained an inkling of self-awareness (one of EQ's four domains).

I encouraged Jeff to build on that inkling by observing himself and others at work. I asked him to notice his reactions to other people and their reactions to him. When did he feel irritated or frustrated with coworkers? What exactly irritated or frustrated him? How did he react? And what was the outcome of that default behavior? Did he become less irritated? Did the person then produce what he wanted the way he wanted it? Or not? I told him he didn't have to do anything about his behavior just yet, simply note it.

Slowly over time, Jeff saw for himself how his irritation and frustration caused hesitation in others. They avoided him. If they had to work with him, they did the minimum they could get away with. Even more worrisome, they were afraid to approach him with questions or to discuss mistakes, exposing him to liability because of poor supervision. Through this exercise, his social awareness (another of EQ's four domains) sprouted to join his growing self-awareness.

As his cadre of awarenesses took their place in his thinking, he realized that by adjusting his behavior (aha, self-management), he could evoke more genial reactions. Over time, Jeff experienced for himself that his being considerate of how others feel made a huge impact on how they felt about him (finally, relationship management), which in the end was a more effective way to go about business and accomplishing his goals.

During one of our sessions, Jeff told me he'd earned a special credential that no one else in his law firm had ever acquired. As I congratulated him, he interrupted me and told me he wasn't looking for congratulations. He wanted to use our session to create a plan for announcing the award at work and how to approach it on social media. He told me that at first, he'd been eager to announce it and almost acted on that impulse. But then he realized it might come off as boastful or condescending because of how he'd treated his colleagues in the past. He wanted to find a way to let people know without seeming like a show-off.

This marked a huge uptick in Jeff's EQ. On his own, he showed awareness of others' hot buttons. Instead of just saying what was on his mind, he thought about how people might feel and respond to his news. He even appreciated and cared that they might not be rooting for him because of his past behavior. Most of all, he understood the situation needed to and could be managed simply by employing some consideration and social skill. Then he could create a win-win outcome for himself and his employer by mindfully rolling out the news and allowing the firm to capitalize on it strategically as well, since Jeff's accomplishment opened opportunities for new work.

Weeks later, Jeff once again showed his growing prowess at self-awareness and self-regulation as others in his office were demonstrating their own lapse in EQ and soft skills. As Jeff was preparing for paternity leave, he was getting all kinds of pushback, including disparaging comments from higher-ups in the firm. A partner even commented to Jeff, "Isn't that what your wife's mother is for?"

Needless to say, after several days of this, Jeff was fuming. But he managed to resist exploding (at least until we spoke). After validating how extremely inappropriate that partner's words were, I asked Jeff to consider what was making these adults act out like children when it came to the subject of paternity leave. What did he think they were really worried about? And what might he be able to do to appease their fear?

In true Jeff fashion, he took those questions straight to the offending partners—though now he knew to couch his questions in ways more likely to get the answers he was looking for.

After some relationship management through socially deft conversations, he gleaned what the major issue was. The firm depended on Jeff. Remember, he was the associate with "the most billable hours." He had a lot of responsibilities in the firm. They were afraid of being without him because Jeff had done nothing proactively to inform his partners about where things stood with his caseload. Given his previous prickly behavior, some may have avoided simply asking him. Although he had everything covered, Jeff had not effectively communicated with leadership about it, so they didn't know and were worried.

While sticking to his commitment to take paternity leave, Jeff worked to calm their fears. By showing evidence of his preparation and that he had contingency plans in place if something did come up in his caseload, he assured the partners all would be well in his absence. Through his actions and care, Jeff was also acknowledging the partners and their feelings, which acts as a natural balm to any situation whether or not the recipient knows that's what you're doing.

While you should not allow any boss to bully you out of taking a vacation, sick leave, or anything else you've earned, in some situations, it is worth the effort to apply some EQ and soft skills to the situation and dig a little deeper to find out what's behind their poor behavior. Jeff could have called out the partners who challenged him or taken his concerns to human resources, but he decided to see the partners as flawed human beings, much like himself. He decided to chalk their rudeness up to their being highly stressed individuals, something again he could relate to. And he understood he himself had been given a second chance. That's empathy.

With time and practice, Jeff's EQ rose and his social skills sharpened. He thought less about himself and more about others. Not because he wanted to, believe me. The old Jeff was still around. He was still ambitious. He was never going to win "Mr. Congeniality" at the office or be the person you turn to for a shoulder to cry on. But now he saw his ambition as the key motivator to pull out those soft skills and manage his career-derailing behaviors.

Once Jeff understood that having people dislike him was going to get in the way of his career goals, he worked hard to reverse the bad impressions he'd made. He came to understand that his resistance to making friends at work was counterproductive to his prospects. He grasped that upping his EQ was a critical piece of a successful career strategy and honing his soft skills would allow his hard skills to shine.

Competent lawyers are easy to find. Jeff eventually made partner because he demonstrated skills beyond basic lawyering. By becoming proficient in soft skills, he added immense value to the firm. Which led to what he wanted most—to make a great living and provide for his family.

EXTROVERTS NEED TO WORK ON SOFT SKILLS, TOO

Kyle was the polar opposite of Jeff. He did come to work to make friends—and he made lots of them. Where Jeff was introverted, somewhat taciturn, and all business, Kyle loved socializing and being the center of attention at work parties. Fun loving, rough around the edges, off-color joke telling, a few too many drinks having—that was Kyle.

Kyle was loud and occasionally out of bounds with coworkers. When things didn't go according to plan, he was known to react passionately. When displeased, he could come across as rigid, blunt, defensive, snippy, and sometimes explosive. Often, Kyle allowed disagreements with coworkers to become heated and turn into swearing matches. Afterward, though, all would be forgiven over cigars. In Kyle's mind, no harm, no foul. But there was a foul. His outbursts made everyone in the office, especially the support staff, uncomfortable and anxious.

Like a health crisis, it often takes something going wrong—like losing a client, receiving disciplinary action, getting demoted, or having a favorite assistant quit—to turn our attention to our lack of EQ and our need for soft skills. Also like a health crisis, the warning signs are typically present long before the issue becomes a crisis.

Kyle's wake-up call came soon after he received an email at home one evening. It was a note from a coworker objecting to some decision Kyle had made earlier that day. Kyle ruminated on it all night. The next day, before his colleague had even set down his briefcase, Kyle pounced, telling him everything that was wrong with his argument and with him.

"I felt out of control," Kyle told me later. He referred to the interaction as his "soliloquy," because it was not a conversation. "I didn't listen at all. I didn't even give him a chance to speak." Suddenly, he saw how damaging his explosions really were to the whole office and that sharing a cigar wasn't going to heal them.

Unlike Jeff, Kyle already had enough self-awareness to understand when he was displaying a career-derailing behavior. He could see that while his famous charm and sense of humor may have been enough to smooth over his outbursts and transgressions with most people in the office, they would never be enough for the partners to see him as leadership material. Truthfully, after that particular uncalled-for rant at his coworker, Kyle said he wouldn't recommend himself for partner. It now was clear to Kyle that if he wanted to advance in his career, he—the consummate people person—would have to up his EQ and hone his soft skills.

To do this, Kyle would need to focus on empathy and impulse control. As we've seen, much of upping your EQ and honing your soft skills comes down to awareness—paying attention to your feelings, the feelings of those around you, and the situation itself. For Kyle, this meant being aware of when his irritation was mounting. In that moment, he needed to shift his thinking and put himself in the other person's shoes. In his head, he needed to argue whatever point was on the table from their side. Then use what he discovered in that argument to choose his next move.

Needless to say, he was imperfect at this—as we all would be. Still, he had to admit that by doing this little exercise in his head whenever he felt angry, his conversations were not only more professional, which is how he wanted to be seen, but they were more productive as well.

About six months into his new practice, Kyle witnessed an associate make a big mistake. "I felt my blood rising," he reported to me. "I wanted to explode. But I took a deep breath, which felt like it was ten minutes long. I thought about the situation from the other associate's point of view. Once I understood their thinking, I was able to forgo my default reaction—'What the f**k are you doing?'—and replace it with a constructive conversation." Using his trademark humor, Kyle explained, "I chose a positive result over an ass kicking."

At the beginning of this work, Kyle thought he was going to have to change completely and declared to me that his goal was to become stodgy. He reasoned that if he were more reserved and less outgoing, it would decrease the amount of trouble he caused. I didn't want Kyle to change who he was, even if that were possible. His natural gifts were extraordinary, and dampening them would have extinguished Kyle.

What Kyle learned through this process is that self-awareness and self-regulation make you more fully who you are—in good ways. You are no longer at the mercy of the world around you, reacting to everything that happens and always paying for the consequences of those reactions. Upping your EQ allows you to more consciously choose your behaviors and act deliberately and with intention, and let those soft skills work for you.

CHECKING YOUR EQ

As Jeff, Kyle, and I all found out, being able to form and manage relationships with other people is inseparable from attaining career goals. As a result, it's imperative that you be alert to your EQ level and which soft skills might need some work. While there are many resources to explore emotional intelligence and strategies to develop these competencies, a good place to start is with these five easy steps:

Step 1: Look to your assessment for clues

Get that personality assessment back out. Look at your natural strengths and weaknesses when it comes to other people. How do you perform in the areas of leadership? Empathy? Impulse control? Or just plain old getting along with others? Note your default behaviors and ask yourself if they are supportive when it comes to your professional relationships. In other words, do they help you or hurt you? Look at your triggers. Do they work against you in the office? What beliefs might you be carrying around that get in the way of developing emotional intelligence or social skills? Do you believe that soft skills are just "touchy-feely" or weak? How is that working for you?

Step 2: Keep an EQ and soft skills journal for two weeks

Note all your interactions and other people's reactions to you. Use this information to become more self-aware and to learn to regulate your behavior so it aligns with your goal for each interaction and for your career.

Step 3: Using your assessment and the data gleaned from your journal, ask yourself these questions:

- Are you aware of your emotions and how they affect other people?
- Are you able to constructively express emotions in a manner that is not hurtful to other people?
- Can you talk about difficult things without being defensive?
- Do you welcome feedback?
- Can you assert yourself and express a point of view in a constructive way?
- Can you attend to, understand, and appreciate how others feel?
- Are you able to delay your impulses to act immediately?
- Can you resolve disagreements without acrimony?
- Are you flexible when it comes to changes in situation or conditions? Or do you freak out? What countermeasures do you have?
- How stress tolerant are you? Do you actively address stress?

If Jeff, Kyle, or I had candidly answered these questions early on in our careers, we may never have faced our derailment moments. We would have known which EQ areas and soft skills needed improvement.

Step 4: Identify someone at work who's good at managing people

Observe how they behave with others above and below them on the organizational chart. Do they make casual conversation? How do they make requests? How do they solve disagreements? Also, observe how others respond to them. Try out behaviors that feel right for you in your own interactions.

Step 5: Finally, take an etiquette class

So often people fail at networking or relationship building because they fear saying or doing the wrong thing. An etiquette or protocol class can build your knowledge of cultural norms and expectations, along with your confidence in social settings. As society changes, rules of etiquette evolve to respond. What is socially acceptable in one decade can be verboten in the next.

Long ago, someone told me to pretend everyone you interact with is your grandmother and treat them as such. When you think about it, that advice comes down to treating the other person with authentic respect, assuming they have wisdom, remaining aware that they know things you don't, and moderating your behavior to meet them where they are.

When it comes to designing your career, the people you meet along the way—whether client, mentor, or coworker—can smooth your path or create hurdles for you. How you relate to them has everything to do with which they choose. By upping your EQ and honing those soft skills, you not only make it easier to get where you want to go, but you also make the ride a whole lot more enjoyable for everyone.

LAW 6 IN BRIEF

- In order to find success and be able to call the shots in your career, soft skills are as important as hard skills. Soft skills are foundational to a successful career.

- It takes more than a JD to practice law. You must also manage clients, direct staff, and get business—all of which require soft skills.
- Employing soft skills—such as empathy, listening, communication, and courtesy—takes emotional intelligence, or emotional quotient (EQ).
- Psychologist and science journalist Daniel Goleman, PhD, divides EQ into four domains: self-awareness, self-management, social awareness, and relationship management.
- Honing your soft skills allows your hard skills to shine.
- Developing your EQ and soft skills doesn't change who you are. Rather, it allows you to be less reactive and more intentional. It's also a nicer way to go through life because you'll have fewer regrets about your behavior.
- Honing your soft skills takes practice. So practice.

Law 7

Make It Rain

> *"If you don't build your dream, someone else will hire you to help them build theirs."*
>
> —*Tony A. Gaskins Jr.*

Despite being a profession built on codification, the practice of law is filled with unwritten laws. One that's rarely mentioned—though your ability to have a career by design depends on it—is you must "make it rain." In other words, if you want to advance in your career and eventually call the shots, you must contribute to the bottom line of your firm or organization in a significant way that makes you valuable and gets you noticed. In private firms, this usually translates into possessing a substantial book of clients. In government and in-house practice, it can mean taking bold action and gathering the influence to further the mission. In either instance, by understanding the currency of your organization, you'll know how to contribute in meaningful ways and create options for yourself.

You should be aware, if you aren't already, that executing this law can sometimes be a catch-22. Doing what you need to do to "make it rain" often causes tension between associates and higher-ups. After all, partners hire associates to do their work for their clients and their agendas—and to do it silently and in the background. Working to build our own client book or our own sphere of influence sometimes conflicts with what others have planned for our time (until it becomes undeniable and begins to pay dividends for the organization). Making it rain is the only way to get the leverage you need and be able to determine the direction of your career. So be careful to go about it thoughtfully and strategically, and in a way that doesn't upset what goodwill you've already fostered with your firm.

WHY CALL FOR RAIN?

If you'd told me when I was a young lawyer that I would one day advise people and write articles—and a chapter in a book—about making it rain (essentially networking, marketing, and sales), I would have laughed, knowing that would never happen. I didn't know the first thing about marketing or networking, let alone asking people for business. And I didn't want to. All that changed, however, the minute the connection between having clients and having choices in my career made itself all too evident.

When I was about ten years out of law school, the firm I worked for was closing. Naturally, I needed to find a new job. I had a decade of hard work, jury trials under my belt, accolades from clients, and great recommendations. My boss was also looking for a place to land. He was leaving with an extensive book of active clients to recommend him. Guess who had better luck attracting a new firm?

Once word hit the street that our offices were closing, my boss and his caseload were courted by numerous firms—though his plan was to be "of counsel" and not do any legal work himself. Before the doors of our law firm were even shut, he received several offers.

At the same time, I, with my excellent résumé and no clients, was having difficulty. When I could get an interview, the "book of business" topic came up again and again. With each rejection, the huge mistake I'd made in leaving signing clients to others and failing to invest in my own practice was more and more obvious.

Firms saw me as an expense. To them, my decade of experience was not an asset; it was a red flag signaling that I'd cost more than someone just out of law school. To their way of thinking—and unfortunately, this calculation is still used by most firms—not only could they pay a new or recent grad less, but they'd also be able to train that person in the firm's preferences. To them, I brought nothing of unique value to the table. I was an interchangeable cog—and an expensive one at that.

In contrast, my boss was a walking revenue stream. His caseload would increase their bottom line on day one. Bringing him on board would be seen as a windfall for their firm. Even if he didn't bill a single hour.

A lawyer without clients or the ability to make things happen is like a cupboard without food. You can't do any work unless someone else stocks your shelves. You are left to sit there waiting for someone else to feed you. So, it should be no surprise when you are regarded and treated as just another mouth to feed.

If you don't make it rain, you will never gain the leverage needed to take control of your career. You will remain an underling, subject to hitting salary caps or being downsized at any time. I learned the hard way that without my own "rain," someone else would always be deciding if I had a job, what I did all day, and where my career could go. This circumstance is all too common in the legal field. I get calls often from lawyers who are ten, even twenty years in practice and have no clients, no network, no prospects.

When I finally was hired by a firm, I vowed I'd never be without leverage again. From that day forward, I'd make it my business to bring in business. As luck would have it, my new firm had a business coach. I made an appointment immediately and still use what I learned from him to this day.

WHERE RAIN COMES FROM

What are the most memorable cases from law school? *Palsgraf v. Long Island Railroad Company*; *Pennzoil v. Texaco, Inc.*; *International Shoe Company v. State of Washington*; *Gideon v. Wainwright*; and so many more. The names are iconic. Burned into our brains forever. We study and learn every detail of these cases—the arguments on both sides, the outcome, and how that outcome reverberates in our society today.

But are we ever taught how the lawyers who handled these cases came to acquire their clients? How did Helen Palsgraf learn of and then select the attorney who would represent her against the Long Island Railroad in her famous chain-reaction personal injury case? What did counsel for International Shoe do to land such a lucrative client and big case?

While learning how these attorneys won their clients may not be important to creating a successful legal argument, it's of utmost importance to your creating a successful legal career.

Making partner, being promoted, or having a lucrative practice isn't like hitting puberty. It doesn't just occur. Yet, no one I knew in law school was thinking about building a book of clients or building the influence necessary to create and then push an agenda. There was no class titled "Making It Rain." We didn't know where clients came from.

Like file folders, paper clips, and subpar coffee, most of us figured clients and career-making agendas would be provided with the job. But as you know by now, clients don't simply appear. Someone in the firm needs to go out and get them. And the people who do are highly valued.

Clients come from networking, marketing, and, yes, sales—three words that turn off a lot of lawyers (and a lot of people, for that matter). One of my law school classmates complained bitterly about the marketing push at her big law firm. "I didn't go to law school to make cold calls," she said. What she really meant was, "It's not my job to worry about business." What she failed to see was that private practice is an entrepreneurial endeavor. So, if you are in private practice, it literally is your job to worry about the business side of things, especially if you want to be considered for partnership or open your own practice (i.e., business).

I once complained resentfully to my boss when I saw the large referral fee going to an outside lawyer who sent us a huge case that I'd worked for years resolving. "She didn't do anything!" I protested. To which he replied, "She did everything. She brought us the business."

Similarly with in-house and government practice, contributing to the currency of your organization—prestige and influence—heightens and expands your potential and possibilities. Prestige and influence aren't just handed to you when you are hired or when you do assigned work—no matter how great a job you do. Prestige and influence come when you create the circumstances that bring them your way, when you make things happen that wouldn't have happened otherwise.

When I was general counsel to a school district in distress, I couldn't generate revenue. But I could propose and take an innovative step that would reduce expenses while better serving our constituency. I put legal services out for competitive bidding for the first time in many years. The process procured excellent law firms that could handle our work for much lower rates than we'd been paying without question for many years. Ultimately, my decision saved the school district close to a million dollars in legal fees and costs in the first year alone. I made it rain. If you are in a non-revenue-generating position, think about how you can reduce expenses and add value.

RAIN CAN'T HAPPEN IN A VACUUM

Whether you are building a client book or a book of game-changing policies and initiatives, you must know how to market and sell your services and ideas, and you must have a receptive network in which to do that marketing and selling.

Again in my position as general counsel to a school district, I had a chance, along with my colleagues, to meet and be photographed with the governor of Pennsylvania. Because of the governor's presence, the event and my department would make the news. It would also be an opportunity for our agenda to have the governor's attention, if only for a moment. I was on the leadership team, having been handpicked for my role by the governor's deputy secretary of education—and this could have been a chance for me to demonstrate leadership.

Everyone in my office went, of course. The entire leadership team. I told myself I was too busy. The school year was starting, and we had transportation and food service contracts needing my attention. As I watched my colleagues file out the door, I felt a bit like Cinderella.

I regretted my decision to stay at my desk that day, and believe me when I tell you how important it is to lift your nose from your legal work and participate in the world. It's like Mother Goose says, "This little piggy went to market, this little piggy stayed home." I was the little piggy who stayed home, when going out might have provided opportunities for me and the school district. I'll never know. What I do know for sure is the hour or so I might have lost to that event wouldn't have made any difference for the school district. My staying behind did not progress anything in a meaningful way and doing so held me back.

Choosing to stay home (i.e., eating lunch at your desk, skipping events, doing only the work in front of you) instead of going to market is choosing not to have a noticeable, quantifiable impact. And that's fine, as long as you understand the relationship between hiding and becoming a secret. One leads to the other. And there are no clients, no power, no influence, and no opportunity to be found when you are a secret.

You can't make it rain from behind your desk. If you are interested in having career options, you and your work must become visible. You can't be valued if you aren't seen. You can't bring in business if no one knows you. To make it rain, you have to stretch beyond the confines of a job description, the usual working hours, and your comfort zone.

HOW TO MAKE IT RAIN—GATHERING THE CLOUDS

Jesse came to coaching because his job search wasn't getting any traction. The reasons why are going to be all too familiar to you by now. His résumé was stellar—top of his law school class, law review, time as a clerk for a state supreme court judge, and he'd now been with a midsize, well-respected law firm for seven years. Much like our old friend Chris in "Law 4: Curate Your Career," like me in my first jobs out of law school, and maybe like you, Jesse hadn't put much (meaning not any) effort into positioning himself for what's next. Jesse was honestly surprised that no one in his firm was ushering him toward a door marked "partner" or even pointing the way. When Jesse thought about his future, he wondered, *When will they make me partner?* Not, *What can I do to deserve partnership?* He felt his gifts were going unnoticed, though he'd done nothing to put them out in front.

Once in coaching, Jesse's personal and situational assessments made clear why he wasn't that valuable on the job market. Everything about him that might recommend him to a firm, which might make him stand out, was well in the rearview mirror. Just like in any business, the law firms he was applying to were focused on the road ahead. Even with no clients, simply demonstrating marketing knowledge, acumen, and effort would have helped, but Jesse hadn't thought to do that.

Jesse now understood that if he wanted to make partner at his current firm or be attractive to another firm or have any options at all, he had to make himself valuable. Nobody was going to do it for him. And the surest way to be of value is to add value, to make it rain.

Before it can rain, however, you have to ready the climate. And that comes down to three steps.

Step 1: Market and network

Potential clients can't choose you and people in the community can't recommend you if they don't know who you are or what you offer. So, take your cues from Chris and follow the networking plan in Law 4. Put in the work to build your network and market yourself and your services, become known in your community, and let people experience you and what you can do.

Step 2: Develop a marketing mindset

Just like you did in law school, train your brain. But now train it to look for opportunities to offer your services. Learn to see the world through marketing-colored glasses. Listen to people. Be honestly interested in them. Be curious. Empathize. In other words, lean into those soft skills you developed in "Law 6: Hone Your Soft Skills." Understand that making the sale isn't always about making it on the spot but about building trust through relationships.

Step 3: Ask for their business

In the end, making it rain comes down to "the ask" and closing the deal. Lots of us see this as the hard part. However, the more you invest in Steps 1 and 2, the easier Step 3 becomes. When done well, these three steps set up a logical sales funnel through which the clients or the influence you seek naturally flow to you. For a professional service provider—like a lawyer—the ask isn't a hard ask. It's a process of building relationships and educating. It's getting to know your clients or constituents to the point where you can anticipate their needs and then guide them to the most advantageous outcomes for them. You may need to practice developing relationships to the point where you can easily ask for business and feel confident that you really do offer value and are not a pest.

For instance, I have a relationship with a personal stylist at Macy's. Sometimes she texts me a picture of a sweater or dress and writes something like, "I picked this out for you. I love it." Is my reaction to this, "How dare she annoy me with her selling"? No! I appreciate so much that she knows my preferences, thought of me when this item came in, and alerted me to it. She wants to sell, of course, but the approach—or ask—is one of service. I like that and often buy what she picks out for me.

WHEN YOU'RE STILL AFRAID TO GET WET

If you are still feeling reluctant about marketing, networking, and making the ask—take a minute to ask yourself why. If you are giving yourself well-thought-out "reasons," I invite you to think again.

All three steps to making it rain ask us to put ourselves out there, to expose who we are and what we want (their business or support), with no guarantee of acceptance. That's a vulnerable spot for a human being. As human beings, when we find ourselves in a vulnerable spot, we often play mind games to put ourselves at ease, cover up our fear, and justify avoiding whatever is making us uncomfortable.

But to avoid making it rain is to avoid the opportunity to have a career by design. If you want to have a say in your career, you need to put the games away and align your actions with your goals—even if doing so makes you feel vulnerable at first.

Here are a few of the most common mind games we "rain-avoid-ant" lawyers like to play. If you see yourself in any of these, ask yourself what you gain from it and what better opportunity might be had by letting it go.

The Anti-Marketer

Some lawyers (and many people) believe *sales* is a dirty word. Until the 1970s, it was illegal for lawyers to advertise their services. Even when it became legal, however, many attorneys continued to feel marketing was beneath the profession and beneath them. Some of those lawyers created cultures in firms that prevail to this day.

If you're still entertaining this antiquated idea that actively prospecting, pitching, and asking for work isn't lawyerly, wake up and look around. Notice the opportunity passing you by. Lots of lawyers don't have this attitude. They are out there actively vying for and getting work that could be yours.

You can't place yourself above the world and expect to have an impact in it. To get the work you want, you have to ask for it. And just a note here, if you have structured your sales funnel right, you won't ever feel like a pushy salesperson. You'll feel like a professional who has the knowledge, talent, and experience to help someone in need.

The Reluctant Marketer

Many lawyers are all about marketing, networking, and selling, as long as someone else is doing it. This was absolutely my preferred way of thinking, until I had my epiphany and realized this hesitancy was dooming me to a default career. I was thin-skinned, as many lawyers are. I told myself that asking for business was bothering people or putting them on the spot. The truth was I didn't think I could tolerate the embarrassment of being turned down.

By acknowledging this fear and examining it from several angles in my mind, I was able to reframe it. In the end, I came to see "not asking" as "not caring." With that, making the ask became a valuable service to my potential client, not a bother. If I got a no, that would be okay. I gave them my best. Over time and with some practice, I became more comfortable with self-promotion and asking for business.

The Perfectionist Marketer

Making it rain is ultimately about human interaction. There is nothing perfect about interactions between people, and there never will be. So if you find yourself putting off promoting or asking for business or support until everything is perfect, know that while you're waiting on perfection, others are jumping on your prospects.

To make it rain and gain all the career advantages that come with it, you need to come out from behind your perfectionist attitude, market imperfectly, network imperfectly, and sell imperfectly.

The Too-Busy Marketer

"Not having enough time" is another avoidance mind game. We make time for things that are important to us. If having options when it comes to your future is important to you, making sure you make it rain should be a regular and an essential part of your workweek. Plan activities in advance that you can do when you have a few spare minutes—like reaching out to current and prospective clients with a phone call or email.

HELP IS EVERYWHERE

You may not fear marketing at all, but you don't know how to do it or where to start. If, after debunking all these mind games, you still find yourself hesitant when it comes to making it rain, consider some formal sales training. Marketing, networking, and selling are all skills that can be learned and are taught in a wide variety of ways.

Start by finding out what, if any, resources are available at your firm. If there aren't any, ask for what you need. Identify who in your office excels at sales and ask them to mentor you. Make it known that you are interested in every aspect of the sales process and looking for opportunities to observe it.

If you don't find what you are looking for at work, make the investment in these necessary skills yourself. Sign up for a class or engage a business coach. Read books, articles, and blogs about marketing. Follow thought leaders on social media whose approaches are aligned with yours. The return on this investment will be well worth your time, effort, and any money spent.

PLAN FOR AND MEASURE RAIN

Once lawyers commit to making it rain, the next hurdle is deciding exactly which marketing and networking activities to engage in. There is no deficit when it comes to what you "could do" in the marketing and networking realm—especially now with seemingly endless online opportunities. The question is which tactics will be most effective and most efficient for you.

Begin your planning by thinking through these five foundational areas first. Once you have clarity on them, you'll know better which actual strategies and tactics to put in place to bring on the kind of rain you want. Plan also for where work is going when you get it. Capacity is an issue marketers must be attuned to. It pays to think ahead so you're not scrambling for help when the new work comes in.

Area 1: Know who your client is

The biggest waste of time and effort is courting business that's not ideal for you—or worse, becoming known for an area of practice you are not interested in. You can prevent both by knowing who your ideal client is, who you want to serve, and who you serve best. Then make sure you target your messaging, marketing, and networking accordingly.

You can go as far as creating an ideal client avatar with identifying and relevant information, including demographics. Write out their problems and pain points. List where your ideal clients turn for industry information, what organizations they belong to, which conventions they attend, what social media they use—and consider how best to have a presence there. Set up alerts for issues they care about so you can email them with useful information.

When you know your client, you can consistently position yourself to meet their needs. Also, you are more likely to recognize them when you meet them. Potential clients are more likely to identify you as someone who can help.

Area 2: Have an elevator speech

In addition to knowing who your client is, you should know what you do for a living . . . and be able to tell people in thirty seconds or less. This might seem obvious, but most people can't do it. Not only is the elevator speech the pinnacle of efficient messaging, but the process of figuring it out, writing it, and memorizing it clarifies your target market and their needs. All of which will help you streamline your marketing and networking.

Area 3: Get the most from your current clients

Your current clients already know and trust you. You've already identified them as ideal clients. Make sure you use them as both the ongoing revenue and referral source they are. Stacy, who you met in Law 1, got a $30,000 engagement from simply picking up the phone and checking in with a current client.

Warning: If you are servicing another lawyer's clients, you may want to have a conversation about origination credit (or whatever system your firm uses) before you endeavor to bring in more business.

One of the most discouraging, disincentivizing, and demoralizing strategies law firms employ is a rigid "fruit of the poisonous tree" analysis to origination credit. This both stifles and kills off entrepreneurial spirit at its roots.

Area 4: Use your network

If you are going to go to the effort of networking, be sure to have a plan to use your network. Think about what kind of relationships would be most advantageous for you. For instance, of course you want to build relationships with ideal clients. But you might also want to seek out professionals in different businesses who serve the same clientele. You can refer clients to them and vice versa.

In that same vein, maybe you want to build relationships with other attorneys who practice in different areas of the law. As you refer appropriate clients to them, you position yourself as a connector. Connectors tend to get more referrals than others because they are . . . connected.

If someone calls you with a legal problem in an area of law you don't practice, take it upon yourself to help. Maintain a list of lawyer friends in common areas of law that people call about—wills, divorce, real estate—and make introductions so the client feels taken care of and your referral source gets a client delivered to their door. If you don't know a lawyer in the field sought, find a few reputable names to pass along. This way you become a go-to person for legal problems, whether they fall into your area or not.

Area 5: Set goals. Evaluate. Tweak. Repeat.

So simple. So important. And so rarely done. If you don't set goals, how will you know that your efforts are paying off? Know what you want from marketing and networking. A certain number of clients per quarter? Meeting an influencer who can help your cause? Hitting a revenue target? Hitting a budget target? You decide what "make it rain" means for you and set goals to achieve it.

As you set your goals, also set up a plan to assess your efforts and hold yourself accountable. Did you meet your goals? Are the goals you set the right ones? Are the marketing, networking, and sales tactics you're using yielding the outcomes you want? Depending on your findings, tweak your goals and tactics to improve performance.

You decide what you want to measure, and then measure it on a regular basis, maybe quarterly. Keep track of your successes and make sure you take credit for them. Reward yourself for the hard work. The brain recognizes the relationship between effort and reward.

A NEVER-ENDING CONVERSATION

Rainmaking is not advertising. You don't just put up a billboard and count the calls coming in. Marketing and networking are long games, with an element of mystery. They require constancy. Just like diet and exercise, the payoff in marketing and networking comes with steady investment over time.

Jesse began to get clients because he began trying. It is that simple, but it's not easy. He had to shift his thinking to prioritize this nonbillable activity and find time for it. He had to be patient (not a strong suit of his) because results didn't happen overnight. But once his efforts began to show results, he built on that momentum. Marketing became almost second nature to him.

I have never seen a lawyer make a strong, consistent effort at marketing who did not increase their book of business. Being able to make it rain creates freedom over time. Loyal clients follow their lawyers, not their law firms, generally speaking. Changemakers in-house and in government work attract opportunities to do even more consequential work.

Occasionally, a client confides in me that fate brought us together. That I just happened to be standing at the career crossroads when the client arrived there looking for a coach. I always smile when I hear that because it wasn't fate, but I love that it seems that way. But no. It was me. Showing up again and again until the time came when someone was looking and there I was. I will continue to be there because making it rain is a never-ending conversation with the world, with former clients, current clients, and future clients.

LAW 7 IN BRIEF

- If you want to have a career by design, you have to be of value. And to be of value, you have to make it rain. This goes for in-house and government lawyers, as well as for those who work in private practice.
- You can't build clients or influence from behind your desk. You can't be valued if you aren't seen. You can't bring in business if no one knows you.
- Marketing, networking, and sales aren't second nature to most lawyers, but they are skills that can be learned. If you find you are reluctant to make it rain, find a mentor, a class, or a coach to help you.
- Making it rain comes down to three steps: (1) marketing and networking, (2) developing a marketing mindset, and (3) asking for business.
- Have a plan for making it rain. Set goals. Measure your progress. Tweak as necessary.
- Making it rain is not a one-and-done proposition. It requires constancy and attention.

Law 8

It's Not Too Late

> *"Twenty years from now you will be more disappointed by the things that you didn't do than by the ones you did do."*
> —*Mark Twain*

U nless you are reading this book on your deathbed (and let's face it, even my mother would not have bothered with it then), it's not too late to make a meaningful change in your life or your career. I would argue that even on the verge of death, there is still time to forgive, to love, to be grateful. I've seen that. When it comes to your life and your career, there's always time and the need for evolution. Always evolve—which makes Law 8: It's Not Too Late imperative to a career by design.

In Law 3, we explored the danger of doubling down on past decisions, and how when we give in to the sunk cost fallacy, we allow our past to determine our future. "Too-late" thinking is the other side of that hollow coin and just as damaging to our careers. It makes a converse but equally fallacious assumption that there's not enough time left in our lives to invest in and accomplish what we desire.

Typically, when we assume it's too late to do something (without investigation or inquiry), we are basing that conclusion on a comparison between our current age and the customary age of people doing the thing we want to do. For instance, most people settle on what area law to practice while still in law school or when they go after or get their first job.

My guess is that you—and the other attorneys attracted to this book—have been out of law school for more than a few years. You've experienced the legal profession as it was handed to you, and you know in your bones there must be a way to practice, a way that could make the job more invigorating, more satisfying. After working through the laws in this book, you might even know what that looks like for you.

Instead of working toward making that career your reality, you tell yourself it's too late for you. If you change it up now, you will "fall behind," unable to ever catch up with your peers. You tell yourself, "If I were (fill in the blank) years younger, maybe it would be worth it. But my ship has sailed."

Here's the thing—life isn't a contest with our peers. When one day you find yourself on that proverbial deathbed, nobody is going to pull out a chart of everyone you went to law school with to see who won life. Right now, you have many working years still ahead. If you make a new investment in your career today, all those years are likely to be a whole lot happier. It's up to you to decide what that's worth.

TIMING ISN'T EVERYTHING

A dear friend of mine likes to say, "Timing is everything in life." Of course, timing can be a friend in some instances and a foe in others, but it is never everything. Timing is just one factor to consider.

Timing can matter. If you know that a business prospect just had something great happen, the timing would be perfect for reaching out to congratulate them and perhaps ask how you can be helpful. Conversely, if you know a client had a setback, the timing might not be right to ask for more work, but reaching out in a different, supportive way could be a way to connect. Those are instances of appropriately gauging what the other person is experiencing (using your soft skills) and how you can best respond to and respect the situation.

There are situations, however, when we lean on timing as if it were the Holy Grail, when it isn't even a factor at all. It's a convenient excuse. We decided for our own comfort that there's a timing problem. "It's just bad timing," we explain to ourselves and anyone who'll listen to us.

When I was a kid, growing up in Philadelphia, I always ran for the bus. It was like a game. I'd see it coming down 54th Street and race to meet it as it crossed City Line Avenue. I'd jump aboard, sucking air and sometimes grabbing on to the door as the #44 bus was pulling away from the stop. When I missed the bus, it wasn't bad timing. It was bad planning. I didn't leave the house early enough.

"Too-late" thinking has a black-and-white quality to it, with no room for the gray. Either/or. Win or lose. This can be an easy mind trap for lawyers, who due to the nature of their work, have that win-lose focus. Life tends to be more malleable than that. Even court deadlines can be continued using the right approach and following the proper procedure. "Too late" uses a quantifiable unit (time) and renders it subjective. Unless the train, plane, or bus has left, it's not too late. Sometimes you might find that they're running late, too.

When we believe that timing is everything, it can become a crutch and a reason not to move forward in our lives. We then chalk up our immobility to an invisible infiltrator, an invidious invader in our plans—the passage of time. In essence, we procrastinate our way out of accountability. We can't help it if it's now too late to act, right?

Well, let's question the evidence.

Sarah was a paralegal in a Philadelphia insurance company. Like many clients, she came to coaching thinking she wanted one thing—to transition to another field of law—when what she really wanted was something else.

As always, we started with an assessment, which made it clear why she wasn't enjoying her current work. Sarah was high in altruism and affiliation, loved academic activities and education, was sociable and sensitive. These qualities did not mesh well with her current role at an insurance company. Her work there was highly repetitive, largely done in isolation, and often involved challenging a deserving person's right to financial compensation. Even though she didn't go to court, she was part of the denial process, and she didn't like that.

As we worked to identify other areas of law that would provide the variety and interaction more suited to her, I got the feeling that nothing in any legal realm appealed to her. Still, she dutifully selected a few areas of practice to research. But she kept showing up to our sessions week after week having taken no steps toward pursuing a job in a new legal field.

Finally, Sarah had to admit to herself and me what was really going on. There was a career direction she'd always wanted to take but for a number of reasons hadn't. "I've always wanted to be an elementary school teacher," she finally said out loud. But she thought, at 42, that by the time she got a teaching certificate, other teachers her age would already be retiring. She felt it was just too late.

"And if you're not a teacher, where will you be when these people your age retire?" I asked. "Still doing something you hate?"

Sarah reminded me of Seth from Law 3, the young attorney who really wanted to be a science teacher. Where past expenditures (education, training, and the expense of becoming a lawyer) were keeping Seth stuck, Sarah's fear of future investment was keeping her from pursuing her dreams. As I said, two sides of the same hollow coin.

I wasn't surprised Sarah couched her argument in terms of retirement. When you are in a job you hate, retirement is always utmost in your mind. When you are in a job you like, it is not usually something you think about as much or at all. Sarah was envisioning teachers retiring as young as possible because, with her current job, that was her current mindset—get to retirement as fast as you can so you can finally enjoy your life.

Sarah thought a change of practice—different clients and cases— would be enough to get her through the next twenty years or so. But once that avenue was in front of her, she couldn't find the motivation to go down it. She was at the intersection of default and design for sure, finding it hard to accept default, but thinking she'd missed the opportunity to become who she wanted to be.

CHANGING DIRECTION ISN'T EASY

Taking the design route isn't easy for any of us. Sarah would have to complete an unfinished college education and go through the steps of becoming a teacher, some of which are a pain in the butt. She'd also have to keep working as a paralegal the whole time to pay the bills. But within just a few years (well before others her age would be retiring, by the way), she'd have a career she loved and decades ahead of her in her chosen profession.

After giving voice to her desire, Sarah realized she'd made the task seem more monumental than it was. She'd also been allowing naysayers who thought she should stay in a secure working environment (an insurance company) in a stable field (law) to keep her in default mode.

After assessing the situation, Sarah collected some data—she was not yet committing to this career change but thinking about it. How many credits did she still need? Quite a few as it turned out, but not as many as she thought. Could she earn college credit for any of the work experience she had under her belt as a paralegal? Well, she could. How many years until she had her degree and teaching certificate? Not as many as she had imagined. Between deciding and doing, how long would it take for her to be in a classroom? About three years. She'd be forty-five.

THE INVESTMENT-TO-OUTCOME RATIO

With real data, Sarah could weigh the actual choice before her. She could make this three-year investment in herself that would result in the career she'd always wanted. Or she could spend from age forty-two until retirement being a paralegal, which she didn't like. In other words, an investment of three challenging years would yield twenty or more years doing work she could love. That's a pretty good investment-to-outcome ratio.

When we think "it's too late" for us to do something we really want to do, we usually are giving too much weight to the investment part of the equation. We forget to balance our calculation with the expected return on that investment and give that return the weight it deserves in our decision-making.

You may have read about Joan Oliver, the Australian woman who graduated from law school at age seventy-five. She wanted to use her legal training to volunteer for an organization specializing in domestic violence. Some might have said that she was too old to go to law school. That it would take her more years to get her degree than she'd have in practice. But that's not how she saw her investment-to-outcome ratio. With her law degree in hand, she was delighted to have accomplished a longtime goal. Even more valuable to her, she could now spend the rest of her life, however long that was, doing something she found important and meaningful. Timing—the fact that she was seventy-five at graduation—wasn't irrelevant to her, but it didn't stand in her way either.

You should never let it stand in your way. When you find your-self thinking it's too late, ask yourself, "Between now and death, what would I rather be doing?"

BETTER LATE THAN NEVER

When I coach lawyers on business development and they neglect to follow up on a prospect or lead in the time originally planned, they will often say they can't do it now, that it's too late. When I press them, I ask, "Was there a deadline, a request for proposals, or other time-barring restriction?" Usually, the answer is something along the lines of, "What will they think if I call now, after all this time?"

Worrying that someone will think poorly of you is self-defeating because as long as you believe it, you won't act and nothing will hap-pen. Ever. When it could.

Instead of attempting mind reading, turn the thought around to yourself (thoughts you actually can divine). When people call you, do you judge them harshly for not calling sooner if there was noth-ing pressing? Do you dismiss their attempts to reengage? Or are you understanding when someone drops the ball in the networking vol-ley? Most people aren't sticklers when it comes to follow-up, so don't be one yourself. Don't say it's too late. Even if the customary time period for the opportunity did pass, what do you lose by still follow-ing up?

In early March 2020, I had initial meetings with several people about starting a coaching engagement. Then COVID-19 hit. We were in lockdown. Normally I would have followed up with those potential clients within a week or so to see if they wanted to get start-ed. But weeks turned into a month or more. Was it too late to reach back out to them?

Since I don't let my clients use that "too late" excuse, I didn't use it myself. However, when I followed up, I did inject acknowledgment of the changed circumstances. Using my soft skills, I wrote, "I know when we last spoke the world was a different place, but clients of mine have been getting jobs and moving forward. So if you'd like to talk, I'm here." I got only positive reactions to this, and one new client. Turns out it wasn't too late, and there is no bad timing when it comes to compassion or offering help.

When delays in follow-up happen, clients worry about what to say, how to couch the time gap. First of all, it's good to anticipate, prepare, and plan, but not to worry. Worry only excites the part of the brain that subdues problem-solving and goes for comfort. Second, there are lots of avenues to take, including the truth—"I wanted to reach out to you so much sooner, but life got in the way. I'm so glad to be talking with you now." Once you shelve the idea that "it's too late," it's really not that hard.

THE CAREER YOU WANT IS POSSIBLE

As you know by now, I changed my practice after thirteen years in the law—from private civil litigation to in-house government law. Then, at age forty-eight, I began taking steps to transition from being a government lawyer to building a coaching practice so I could help other attorneys find the kind of career satisfaction I'd enjoyed. I was fifty-nine when I started writing this book, my first. By the time it's published, I will be sixty years old. When I was submitting the book proposal, I admit the thought went through my mind, *Is it too late to be a first-time author?*

When I have those thoughts, I think of others who have done amazing things in midlife and old age. Anna Mary Robertson Moses, otherwise known as Grandma Moses, is, forgive me, the grandmother of it's-not-too-late stories. She began painting seriously when she was seventy-eight years old. Her work sold and was exhibited in museums during her lifetime. None of that would have happened if she thought it was too late.

Sylvia Lefkowitz, my mother, was a great role model in this area because she never started any sentence with, "I'm too old to . . ." As she got older and frailer, we urged her to do less, but no way. She did everything she could, up until her very last day in her home, including taking out the trash. She was ninety-three.

I also think of Sarah and Seth overcoming their objections to changing career directions. I love to think of them in classrooms with their students. I think of Seth standing at the blackboard teaching chemistry and Sarah with a circle of children around her, reading aloud. I think of the lives they are touching and influencing with their enthusiasm and energy.

Timing is important, but it isn't everything. Even when we are late, there are still avenues to take. It might be too late for you to try out for the U.S. gymnastics team. But there are lots of meaningful changes we can make to our lives right now. It's not too late for a conversation, an apology, or to choose different thoughts. And it's not too late to make the investment in yourself that results in the career and life you want. We always have the power within us to shift from negative (it's too late) to positive (what's possible).

Regularly questioning everything we think we know about ourselves—our decisions, endeavors dismissed out of hand, whether it's really "too late"—is an invaluable practice. As we move through life, we gain experience. We gain self-knowledge. We change over time and so do our preferences.

My career was only possible because I was open to questioning my reservations, the status quo, and updating the data in my brain, including the way I saw myself and my identity. (Admittedly at first, this "openness" was forced on me by my intense dislike of litigation. But that's okay. It doesn't matter how you get there, as long as you do.)

When I look back over the decades and the various phases of my career, I can credit the pleasure my work has brought me to learning to engage opportunity, to invest in myself, to place value on what I wanted and to go for it—whether or not the thought that "it's too late" was in the back of my mind. I see this in my clients, too, as they begin to experience their career by design.

It is never too late to invest in the life you want. To this day, I have never really thought much about retirement. Because throughout my career incarnations, I've always been evolving and doing work I enjoy with clients I love—and I plan to continue. What better return could there be?

LAW 8 IN BRIEF

- It's never too late to make a change in your career.
- Thinking it's "too late" is a false assumption that there is not enough time left in your life to have what you really want.
- Timing isn't everything. It's just one factor to consider when making a decision.
- If we allow it, "too-late" thinking can become an excuse for not acting.
- "Too-late" thinking is often the product of attributing too much weight to the investment required to make something happen and not enough to the yield that investment will provide. Instead of giving in to "too late" thinking, think investment-to-outcome ratio.
- It is better to be late than to not show up at all in your life. When you do nothing, nothing happens. Ever. When it could.
- No matter what time it is in our lives and career, if we choose to, we can shift our thinking from negative (it's too late) to positive (what's possible).

Law 9

Create an Environment for Change

> *"It takes as much energy to wish as it does to plan."*
> —*Eleanor Roosevelt*

Clearly you've decided something needs to change in your career. As you've held this book in your hands, you've likely also held an image in your mind: the image of how it will feel when you stop living in default mode and move toward a career of your own design.

Many people jump from default to design, from inaction to action by immediately adding more to-do items to their already busy lives. Be careful here. Action without preparation, clear purpose, and direction usually leads to suboptimal results. Whether we like it or not, spackling the walls before painting makes for a smoother coat; warming up before exercising prevents injury; and removing some complications from your life (literally and figuratively) before making a big change makes room for a more successful transformation. Law 9—Create an Environment for Change—shows you how.

MISE EN PLACE OF IT ALL

I used to hate to cook. Mostly because I was a disaster in the kitchen. I'd see a dish that looked delicious in the cookbook, get out the ingredients, start following the recipe, and from there all I'd create was a huge mess. Every time. As onions burned in the frying pan, I'd be feverishly dicing vegetables for the next step, all while looking for my measuring cups or whatever. Rarely did my dish turn out as advertised, and I'd be too embarrassed to serve it and too frustrated to eat it.

One little phrase changed all that: *mise en place.*

A French phrase that translates to "everything in its place," *mise en place* is a process used by chefs. Before cooking, chefs read the recipe in full (imagine that), organize and arrange their workspace and equipment, and then gather and prepare all the ingredients. Whatever a recipe calls for—minced garlic, sifted flour, a tablespoon of this, a half cup of that, and/or a preheated oven—is ready and waiting for them when needed. (You often see *mise en place* at work on cooking shows.)

Employing this one simple practice eliminated the mayhem and mess from my kitchen. The preparation expanded my capabilities. I gained confidence. New things no longer scared me. Cooking became a pleasure. And the quality of my dishes . . . well, I hate to brag, so let's just say there were no more burnt onions.

Mise en place has proven to be an amazing tool in tackling complex tasks beyond the kitchen as well. Whether planting a garden, putting together an argument for trial, or orchestrating a career transition, prepping—putting into order—what you can before you get down to the business of creating something new not only relieves anxiety, but also clears the way for ingenuity and bold action.

Think of it this way: the things that are weighing you down in your current life are only going to impede your progress as you work to move in a new direction. You cannot climb a ladder while clinging to your old baggage. So just as you would remove the rocks before planting a garden, it only makes sense to rid your environment of any obstacles to change before implementing a big one.

When moving a career out of default mode and into design mode, the prep work typically comes down to three tasks: clearing your space of clutter (literally and figuratively); eliminating energy drainers from your life; and fine-tuning your attitude. By the way, as you work toward getting things in order, don't be surprised if things feel a little out of order at first. In general, things tend to get messier before they are resolved. If you've ever walked in on housekeeping in a hotel room, you've seen that firsthand.

CLEARING OUT THE CLUTTER

Most people hire a business coach so they can be more successful in their careers, heighten their professional profile, or increase their income. They are usually not seeking help with clutter. Yet whatever the end goals, often the first issue coach and client tackle is creating physical space for growth to happen. You can't practice *mise en place* if you don't have any "place" to put things.

It is difficult to get things done in an office that's disorganized or overflowing with stuff, or both. You wouldn't strap weights to your body just to make it harder to get around, would you? Then why try to transform your career in a space that constrains your effectiveness?

A lawyer I once worked with had an office that was so messy, you couldn't walk through without sliding on the papers lining the floor. His desk and chairs were piled high with documents, and there were always boxes outside his door. He was highly intelligent, skilled, and knowledgeable. Still, the clutter added extra time to everything and caused him to work longer hours than necessary. His physical environment was choking him, tamping out his ability to efficiently manage his caseload, and creating more of what he did not want—additional hours at the office. Not to mention, a messy office with papers everywhere doesn't exactly instill confidence in the lawyer willing to work in that chaos.

In my own home, I used to spend a lot of time looking for my car keys. Granted, they were usually in one of four spots where I'd habitually dropped them. But those four spots were on two different floors and in four different rooms. Locating my keys made my hectic mornings more hectic—every single day.

One time when I was headed out the door to deliver an important speech—with my hair blown out and in my best outfit—I realized I didn't have my keys. I rushed around the house to look for them in all four spots. Not there. I looked in my hand (just to be sure). Not there. After ten more minutes of frantic searching, I found them on the kitchen counter where I'd set them down with the groceries the evening before. This heart-pounding, sweat-inducing, and hair-deflating experience almost caused me to be late, adding stress to an already anxious situation. When I arrived and was introduced to the event organizers, I was too distracted to make my best first impression.

Our disorganization and clutter cost us. They waste our time and energy. They have a profound effect on our productivity and detract from our reputation. This goes for "organized clutter" as well. Studies show that clutter competes for our attention and thus limits our brain's ability to focus. The very existence of clutter makes people feel less competent, less accomplished, and in a constant state of being unfinished—which keeps us in a state of agitation. Not exactly a supportive environment for transforming your career.

However, when we rid our space of what's no longer needed and know where things are, we make space in our physical environment and in our own heads for the things that matter. With clutter out of the way, it becomes easier to envision plans with clarity, make decisions, and move forward. As my own clients vanquish their clutter, I've noticed they become more focused, optimistic, and creative.

As my client Janine was embarking on a new home-based business, she realized there literally was no space in her house for this new venture. Every room from basement to attic was filled with stuff—most of which she no longer needed, like baby clothes (her youngest child was sixteen). As she put it, "There is no 'me' place in my house."

For Janine, clearing that clutter was the first step in moving into this new phase in her life. By the end of her purge, she was able to claim a whole extra bedroom for herself and her business. She transformed it into a professional, yet comfortable office where she could think, do business, and realize her entrepreneurial dream.

Decluttering and organizing doesn't need to overwhelm you. You don't have to do your whole office or whole house at once. Set your sights on one room or even one file drawer. Then use the feeling of accomplishment you get from organizing that to tackle another area.

If you are one of those naturally organized souls who does have a place for everything and everything is in its place, more power to you. It still won't hurt to take a little time to look at your space and see if there is anything you might want to discard, move, or change before you set out on your new career direction. If you are challenged in this area, as I am, consider hiring a professional organizer.

As for me and my keys, barely making it to my speech on time coupled with a frantic, out-of-control feeling induced a "never again" moment. I was done searching for keys. So, I had some hooks installed by the door and set an intention to always put my keys there. It took some practice. Sometimes I was halfway up the stairs and forced myself to backtrack to the hooks to hang my keys. Eventually it became a habit. With this one little move toward cleaning up my space (and my act), I now save time every day.

CREATING AN ENERGY-POSITIVE ENVIRONMENT

As my story showed, having to search for my perpetually lost keys took more than my time—it stole my energy and impacted my confidence as well. What's most amazing is that for years I put up with this annoying, time-consuming daily ritual. Even though it took so little effort to change it, I tolerated it.

Before you place more demands on yourself—ones that have the potential to advance your life and career—it would benefit you to eliminate demands from your life that have no return on investment. Such demands—or energy vampires, as I like to call them—come in all shapes and sizes. They exist in every area of our lives. They can range from small annoyances to full-blown toxic relationships. And they can be identified by answering one question: What am I tolerating in my life right now?

Thomas J. Leonard, a major contributor to the development of personal coaching and the author of *The Portable Coach: 28 Surefire Strategies for Business and Personal Success,* coined the phrase "eliminating tolerations." He created a master list of 1,001 things to stop tolerating. The list included things such as negative attitudes of coworkers or a boss, clients who cancel appointments at the last minute, inadequate retirement funding, broken things, and so on.

Over the years, when I've asked new clients what they tolerate, their answers have ranged from "email" to "my commute" to "my sister." What all tolerations have in common is they steal our energy and block our personal, professional, and emotional growth. So, it only makes sense to deal with our tolerations and take care of as many as possible before starting our career transformation.

Here, I challenge you to ask yourself what you are tolerating in your life and come up with at least five things. Write a few sentences about how each affects you in the moment and afterward. Then write about what your life might look or feel like if you were able to reduce or remove them. Start with smaller annoyances so you can get a sense of how big a difference removing even those from your life can make.

Say you've been tolerating tight shoes. How does that affect you? The shoes hurt and that makes you irritable. Plus, you can't walk as far in them. How would you feel if you replaced those tight shoes with ones that fit? Your feet would feel a whole lot better and you'd probably be more agreeable, which usually leads to better outcomes. Also, you could pay attention to things other than your smarting feet. Both of these outcomes would add greatly to the quality of your life.

With respect to larger issues of toleration, more introspection is probably needed. For instance, if an energy drainer is a relative, friend, or boss, you may not want to or be able to completely eliminate that person from your life. And you don't have to. By simply realizing the drain, you take back your energy and redirect it toward an energy-saving solution, such as reducing exposure to them.

For example, my client who identified her sister as an energy vampire grasped that spending hours each week on the phone listening to her sibling's problems, which were never acted upon or changed, was a waste of time and took an emotional toll. My client did not want to expend energy on this futile effort anymore, but she also didn't want to remove her sister from her life. So, she decided to reduce the frequency of their calls. This allowed her to still have a relationship and save her precious energy for more productive activities.

Eliminating tolerations doesn't mean you have to eviscerate everything (or everyone) in your life that annoys you. That would not be possible or practical. But you can take charge of your energy and reduce your susceptibility to energy vampires. Remember, vampires must be invited in. You do have some choice when it comes to who, how much, and when.

ENSURE YOUR ATTITUDE IS AN ASSET

You also have a choice when it comes to your attitude and approach to problems. People who are in charge, who take agency over their careers, don't default into whining and complaining when something isn't right. They act. As you prepare to design your career, you want to cultivate an attitude that advances your intentions and empowers you toward your goals.

I have done my share of both whining and complaining. So, no judgement here. Early in my career, I'd complain about anything—bad jobs, micromanaging bosses, plain bagels at the staff meeting. So did most of my coworkers. You've seen the whiner's club in action—staff clustered together griping about clients, partners, and each other. There was a time in my life when if I asked someone how they were and they said, "Can't complain," I'd immediately wonder what was wrong with them.

Where did all that complaining ever get me? Nowhere. Complaining helps no one and solves nothing. It only reinforces what's going wrong, without looking for a way to make it right, keeping us stressed and stuck. Griping positions you as the victim, not the problem solver, and certainly not the leader in your or anybody else's mind. Such an orientation can only weigh you down and set you back as you work to spark change.

Jill, a highly successful attorney, noticed that complaining and whining were part of her office culture, and she all too easily joined in. As Jill put it, "We'd start by grumbling about some mundane irritant like laundry. Then we'd expand into more triggering problems like work or annoying family members."

She credited complaining with others as taking the focus away from herself. "In the moment, it was kind of a relief and a bonding experience with my coworkers," she confessed. But once she returned to her desk, she reported feeling dragged down by the victim mentality. She described it as being left with a negativity hangover that infected the rest of her day.

Luckily, we can shift a negative attitude by simply catching ourselves mid-thought and then realigning our thoughts with our true intentions. In fact, the next time you feel the urge to complain, step back and note it. Become mindful of how complaining makes you feel and how it leaves you. Note also how often you find yourself in the company of others who are complaining. Ask yourself what their complaining is doing for them. What is it doing to you? (It can be like air pollution.) Then shift your focus to one of solving the problem you've been complaining about. Even if you can't or don't solve it, that alone will shift your attitude in a more productive direction.

To promote a more commanding attitude, think of the wisdom I found inside of a fortune cookie: "You can't expect to be a lucky dog if you are always growling." It suggests that we make our luck with our attitude. What you appreciate, appreciates. When applicable, turn your discourse around—either out loud or in your head. For example, replace "I have to walk my dog" with "I get to walk my dog."

And always, always begin and end your days reflecting upon three things you are grateful for in your life. Just as Jill found herself in a domino effect with complaining, so it goes with gratitude. Don't use the same three things every day—spouse, kids, house, done! No, you're training your brain to look for more things to appreciate rather than taking them for granted. Think about the things you never think to actively appreciate, like heat, an encouraging smile, or your cozy pajamas.

Our attitude—how we view and approach the world—can be a huge asset as we embark on transforming our careers. By protecting it from negative influences, we empower it to allow us to see opportunity in every moment.

AS READY AS YOU'LL EVER BE

The goal of Law 9 isn't to create a pristine environment devoid of anything that impedes your career progress—that's simply not practical and certainly not the way life works. Clutter, energy vampires, snarky remarks, and other barriers to success will come and go. What Law 9 can produce is an environment that you make happen and take charge of—not one that happens to you. An environment that is supportive and energy giving. An environment as intentional, as fulfilling, and as dynamic as your career by design.

LAW 9 IN BRIEF

- For best results, create an environment that is conducive to and ready for changes you are about to affect.
- The concept of *mise en place* (everything in its place) shows that it is much easier to achieve success when you prepare for it.
- In career transformation, that preparation characteristically comes down to three things: decluttering your space, quashing what steals your energy, and ensuring your attitude supports you.
- Start with decluttering. Make room in your space and in your head for the goal you are about to embark upon.
- Then become aware of what in your life gives you energy and what takes energy from you (energy vampires). Ask yourself, "What am I tolerating? And what is the impact? What would my life be like without it?"
- Use that awareness to bring more of what energizes you into your life, while at the same time reducing or at least better managing those things that exhaust you with no return for your effort.

- Take on the attitude of a career designer. Stop whining and complaining like a victim. You are not a victim unless you choose to be. Start seeing yourself as a problem solver.
- Just as designing your career is an ongoing process, keeping your environment in a state that encourages that design is ongoing, too.

Law 10

Tend to Your Well-Being

> *"What is a weekend?"*
> —*The Dowager Countess in* Downton Abbey

You've heard the instructions at the beginning of every flight, right? You must secure your own oxygen mask before you can help anyone else, the crew announces.

Yet most of us lawyers exist on too little oxygen for years. We don't get enough sleep or rest. We resist taking breaks from the constant responsibilities we carry on our shoulders for other people. We work through illness. We have no real downtime, recreation, exercise, avocations, and many other things that add up to create a fully dimensional life. Our lives are dominated by work. (Admit it. When you get invited to a party or your spouse brings up a vacation or, if we're being really honest, when there's a family emergency, the first question that runs through your head is, "How will this affect work?")

It's not totally our fault that we think like this. Workaholism in general is seen as a virtue in American culture. Law school and the legal practice simply reinforce that and take it one step further by making it a professional standard—ensuring that those who enter the law with a life eventually end up without one.

Think back to your first semester of law school. The amount of work was insurmountable. That was on purpose. First-year law school curriculum is designed so no one can do it. Let me repeat that. No one can do it. That is why study groups exist. The workload for years two and three can feel just as punishing.

Once in practice, partners and judges take over where professors left off, placing unrealistic expectations on lawyers throughout their careers. Working nights, weekends, holidays, it never stops—and subsequently, we never feel caught up, finished, or done.

LET'S DO BILLABLE HOUR MATH!

I'm not good with numbers. Through client assessments, I've learned that I am not alone here; many lawyers share this trait. Perhaps this is why we lawyers don't think much about the yearly billable hour requirements at law firms before jumping in.

But we should. Because billable hour requirements will run your life in private practice. Targets vary in law firms, but they generally range between 1,800 and 2,000 billable hours per year. Like everywhere else in the law, there are unwritten rules here, too. I once interviewed at a Philadelphia firm that officially required 2,100 hours per year, but I was quietly informed that anything less than 2,400 would not be acceptable. Now in my coaching practice, I hear stories like that every day.

What does it take to bill 1,800 hours in real life? Yale Law School's Career Development Office published a guide titled, "The Truth About the Billable Hour," which can be found on Yale's website. It illustrates what it takes to actually bill 1,800 hours per year.

It turns out, by their calculations and with a caveat, to bill 1,800 hours, you must be at work for 2,434 hours. The caveat as stated in the guide says, "Keep in mind that these schedules do not account for personal calls at work, training/observing, talking with coworkers, a longer lunch (to exercise or shop perhaps), a family funeral, pro bono work (if not treated as billable hours), serving on a Bar committee, writing an article for the bar journal, or interviewing an applicant." This is important because these activities are expected at most firms.

The guide then suggests, "When contemplating offers from firms, ask questions to learn more about their billable hour policies and practices." As associates move closer to partnership, their participation in these nonbillable activities is expected, requiring partners, in many instances, to work harder after achieving that title.

So, what would being at work for 2,434 hours per year require on a weekly basis? Allowing for holidays and vacation, you would be at work for at least 51 hours every week. But what if your firm has higher targets? Many associates are regularly billing 2,200 hours per year or more.

Logging 2,200 billable hours per year takes about 3,058 of actual work hours to achieve and, as of 2022, is not an unusual expectation in the profession. At that rate, with vacation, sick days, and national holidays totaling about four weeks, an average workweek would be 64 hours (and we are not counting your commute). Week after week after week. And let's not forget that in many firms, everybody knows that if you want to get ahead, you need to bill more than the standard. I have clients who bill 2,700 to 2,800 hours annually.

When I was in litigation practice, I remember casually mentioning to colleagues that I was planning to reestablish a favorite hobby in my "free time." My boss overheard and snapped, "Free time? You don't have free time. Your time is my time." His words remain etched in my soul some thirty years later. He wasn't kidding. And his attitude isn't rare.

Being called for trial the day after Thanksgiving or on New Year's Eve, missing the holidays due to work, doesn't surprise any lawyer. Judges don't care what plans, flights, tickets, or reservations we make. We are always expected to cancel and get to work.

LACK OF WELL-BEING IS SYSTEMIC IN LAW

Every year, thousands of new lawyers join this march away from well-being. The situation is so dire that the American Bar Association (ABA) and bar associations across the country began warning about the state of well-being in the legal profession some years ago.

To study the issue and make recommendations for improvement in this area, the ABA created the National Task Force on Lawyer Well-Being. Their 2016 report presents compelling data, including shocking statistics on the high rates of depression, anxiety, chronic stress, and alcohol abuse among lawyers. Other difficulties the report lists include social alienation, work addiction, sleep deprivation, job dissatisfaction, incivility, and work/life conflict.

A 2021 report from the New York Bar Association's task force on well-being had similar findings and made this valid point that anyone who cares about the law and the legal profession should pay attention to: "While the well-being of lawyers may seem like an individual lawyer's problem, the data has been sounding an alarm for the better part of three decades that the training, culture, and economics of law contribute exponentially to the suffering in our profession."

In other words, it's not your fault if you are suffering from the demands of the profession. It was like this when you got here. From what I see in my coaching practice, not much has changed between 2016 and 2021. In the actual workaday world, the topic of personal well-being is brushed aside in most firms and offices. Those entering the profession absorb the attitudes and habits of their leaders, bosses, and mentors, further embedding this "work-above-all-else" posture into the profession.

Recently, a client of mine took the difficult step of confiding in his boss that he's burned out. "We all are," she said, making no further response or taking any action to address or relieve his situation.

Needless to say, this unrelenting expenditure of our energy in one direction—work—exacts a toll on us, our families, our clients, and our profession. You can't be innovative or sharp when you are physically and mentally exhausted. Our well-being is the underpinning of success in life and in our careers.

The national task force report, of course, recommends that stakeholders—judges, regulators, legal employers, bar associations, and legal assistance programs—address the crisis in lawyer well-being. The report suggests that consistent action among those groups could bring transformational change to the legal profession.

I agree. Everyone agrees. But nothing happens. And until something happens—like everything else when it comes to your life and your career—it's up to you to understand the value of your well-being, make it a priority, and invest effort into cultivating it.

Convincing lawyers of this is not always easy. That's why "Tend to Your Well-Being" is the last law I introduce here, though it is arguably the most important law and indisputably foundational to a career by design.

When clients come to coaching, most aren't in the right mindset to address what to them appears to be a non-work-related subject like well-being. They want to effect change in their careers, right now. They are anxious to make partner or open their own firm or change their area of practice. Even when they are totally burned out, they believe immediate change is the answer to all of their problems.

Convincing them of the importance of downtime or making room in their life for a hobby or spending more time enjoying themselves can be a hard sell at that point. They don't realize how far out of balance their lives have become or how much that imbalance impacts their effectiveness on the job.

It is not until they've assessed their careers and have done the work of the other laws that their minds open to the importance of self-care and the real value to their career of having more in their life than work.

Remember Jenn in Law 5? She didn't start going to the gym until she gave herself permission for self-care. And that only came as a result of her taking stock and looking at her people-pleasing ways and what they were bringing to her life. When she did attend to her well-being, it led to vast improvements at work, including a big raise and bonus. Putting yourself first really does pay dividends.

So, if right now you are having a little trouble figuring out how tending to your well-being is something worth paying time, effort, and attention to at this stage of your career, know you are in good company. And know that once informed, most of that company caught on to the relationship between well-being and career success quickly.

SO, WHAT IS WELL-BEING?

The national task force report (adopted by the ABA) defines "well-being" for lawyers as "a continuous process whereby lawyers seek to thrive in each of the following areas: emotional health; occupational pursuits; creative or intellectual endeavors; sense of spirituality or greater purpose in life; physical health; and social connections with others." It also recognizes well-being as part of our "ethical duty of competence" to our clients. You have to be well to practice well.

What that comes down to in everyday life is prioritizing your health and yourself.

Remember Gretchen, the overwhelmed family law attorney from Law 1? At our first meeting, Gretchen said, "I feel physically ill from the stress of my office. I get a feeling in the pit of my stomach when I think about work. This is really bad."

Like many of us, Gretchen was raised to make the best of things—work first, everyone else's needs second, her own needs last. So, she ignored her well-being and tolerated a boss who generated a constant stream of perceived "emergencies." Because of who he was and how he saw things, he created a firm culture where everything was treated as urgent—and no one, including Gretchen, ever questioned it.

"Work feels like people are constantly throwing balls at me, and I can't catch them fast enough," Gretchen said. When I asked about her own goals, she said, "It would be nice to not feel sick at work." The only "strategy" she could come up with to reach that goal was to quit the law.

Gretchen's state of burnout was caused by years of being in an office in constant crisis mode and an often false state of emergency—not to mention years of her tolerating the situation and not providing herself the relief she needed.

THE KEY IS NOT TIME MANAGEMENT—IT'S SELF-MANAGEMENT

Well-being doesn't come from tacking more "me time" onto either end of an already too long workday. It comes from managing yourself and your energy. Knowing what's important to you and making sure those things have a place in your life. It's easier said than done, to be sure, but essential for well-being. You cannot make more time. As I said in Law 1, we all get the same amount—168 hours per week. But you can decide what you will and will not do with the time you have.

Gretchen's ability to calm the storm at her own desk and in her own life didn't come from working more hours or from some "work smarter, not harder" efficiency mantra. It came from starting with Law 1 and assessing her situation from a neutral place. With that data front and center, she realized she had more control over her work life than she originally thought and employed that control, no longer defaulting to the demands of others. She began practicing two skills she rarely had used before: asking for help and saying no.

Through prioritizing her well-being, not only did Gretchen obtain her goal of not feeling "sick at work," but everybody else—her boss, her coworkers, their clients, the overall office culture—was better off as well.

Eventually that move toward well-being spilled over into the rest of Gretchen's life. Without a constant drain on her system from work, she had the bandwidth to take some courses in things that interested her outside the law. She even joined a few social groups and started having fun again—which further reduced her stress levels.

These new activities expanded her world, which expanded her mind. She became more interesting, more content, happier. She had more energy at work. She was more open to new ideas and was more pleasant to be around. People wanted to work with her. That made her more valuable to the firm, giving her more leverage to call the shots than she'd had as a harried worker who always said yes.

That's what tending to your well-being can do for a career, and one of the many reasons it's imperative for anyone who wants a career by design to prioritize well-being.

FINDING YOUR WAY TO WELL-BEING

There's a myth in the world about "having it all." It says you can pursue a high-powered career, along with parenting children attentively or taking care of aging parents (or both)—all while maintaining good social relationships and your physical, spiritual, mental, and emotional health. Even if it were possible, it sounds grueling.

When people talk about having it all, I think what they are really talking about is having everything they want plus everything their friends have and everything society thinks they should have, even if they themselves don't want those things.

Tending to your well-being begins with leaving the myth of having it all behind and shooting instead for having everything that's important to you. Obviously, when you spend time doing things that are meaningful to you, you feel better and are better.

But first you have to know what's important to you, then fill a majority of your life with those things.

At the risk of sounding like a broken record at this point, the road to well-being begins with assessment. Luckily, like Gretchen, you've already done the bulk of this work in Law 1. Simply return to both your personal and situational assessments, and mine them for data about your preferences and values.

Pay special attention to how you scored your "Eight Domains of Life" assessment, those eight domains being career, family and friends, significant other/romance, fun and recreation, health, money, personal growth, and physical environment. In which domains did you give yourself a high score in satisfaction? In which could your satisfaction be better? Do your high and low scores line up with what you value as important in your life?

The point of reanalyzing these assessments with an eye toward your well-being is not to put more on your to-do list. It is to provide a baseline of your overall well-being right now and to give you some guidance as to which areas to focus on to improve it.

Next, take the data from these assessments and apply it to the following six areas the national task force identified as necessary for lawyers to achieve well-being:

Area 1: Emotional health

Take a moment and ask yourself how you feel. Really. Overall. Are you content? Anxious? How do you feel about your job? About your life? Where are the stressors in your life right now? What gives you energy and makes you excited to wake up in the morning? Work? Family? A new project? None of these? All of these?

After you identify what makes you feel good and what is producing anxiety in your life, turn to your situational assessment (like Gretchen did) to gather some data. Then ask what realistically you can do to relieve the stressful situation. And how you can increase what energizes you.

In addition to the above exercises, here are some simple and general practices that I use and recommend to clients to enhance emotional well-being:

- Adopt a gratitude practice where you reflect for five minutes or so each day on three things you are grateful for. Focusing on what's going right for you gives your brain a breather from stress and teaches it to look for and recognize the good.
- Make a habit of reading books, blogs, and magazine articles, listening to podcasts, or watching videos where experts share strategies for growing happiness and bringing more optimism into your life.
- Journal daily to process unexpressed emotions. Often through writing, I'm able to uncover the root causes of my frustration, so I can resolve it or at least acknowledge it, so it doesn't eat at me. Journaling gets my agitation out of my head and onto the page, where it can be examined.
- Use meditation to practice mindfulness and self-soothing. If you think it's impossible to sit still, I invite you to try it for thirty seconds. If that still frightens you, try a moving meditation such as yoga or a hike in the woods—without headphones.

If you have trouble evaluating how you feel or don't see a way to bring things into your life that support your emotional health, consider making an appointment with a therapist.

Area 2: Occupational pursuits

With your situational assessment (Law 1) in hand once again, look at the data, feel what you feel, and ask yourself, "Is my current job satisfying?" You are now looking at occupation through the lens of well-being rather than advancement, status, salary, and so on, and asking yourself if it's contributing or detracting from your desired state.

What is within your power to make your workday better? How can you use what you do every day to shed light on your next steps? What is working for you that you'd like to incorporate into your next move? What isn't working that you want to eliminate in your next job?

With these questions answered, consider doing a new situational assessment to help you determine what's possible for you now and how to go about achieving it.

Area 3: Creative or intellectual endeavors

When was the last time you did something creative or learned something new—not for work, but for the sake of knowledge, because you were interested in it? A year into my first job, I realized I hadn't read a novel in twelve months. I was an English major and devoured books. This was not a healthy sign.

Don't let this happen to you. Right now, make a plan to make something with your hands, pick up an instrument and play, or pursue any interest of your choosing outside of work.

To stay supple and in prime condition, your brain and body need variety and new ways to be creative.

Area 4: Sense of spirituality or greater purpose in life

Because our legal minds have been trained to be so analytical and factual, spirituality and greater purpose can be a difficult area for lawyers. If you do feel untethered or lost when it comes to this arena, look to what you value and anchor to that. Simple ways to bolster your sense of connection and purposefulness are to volunteer for something you care about, mentor someone, or do an act of kindness.

Area 5: Physical health

Your body is the vehicle that carries you through life. So, taking care of it is not up for debate—yet, how many of us spend our lives hunched over our desks, surviving on takeout and coffee?

Maintaining physical health is essential to having a career by design. Your physical health impacts your ability to function every day in every way. Exercise, adequate sleep, proper nutrition, and maintaining a healthy weight comprise the necessary routine maintenance. Build them into your life now.

If you are not sure where to start, ask for help. There's lots out there. See your doctor for an overall picture of your health. Hire a registered dietician to optimize your eating habits. Get a personal trainer to set up an exercise routine that fits easily into your life. If your physical environment is overloaded with clutter, it may be impeding your ability to address anything. In that case, consider a professional organizer (as suggested in Law 9).

Area 6: Social connections

In my first year of law school, my boyfriend tried to break up with me because I never had time for him. When he finally found me, with my nose in a casebook, to tell me this, I told him I didn't have time to talk about it and asked if it could wait until after finals. I'm embarrassed to say this behavior didn't stop at graduation. As a young lawyer, I consistently damaged friendships by canceling plans whenever work called, being too stressed to keep a promised date, and failing to keep in touch with friends until I didn't have many.

The relationship between isolation and depression is well-documented. If the only relationships you value and make time for are at work, you are jeopardizing your well-being. Personal relationships sustain you during bad times and uplift you during good ones. You can count on them to be there for you in a way that work never can or will. So, tend to them.

After evaluating your feelings and behaviors in all six of these areas, come up with a plan to improve your well-being wherever you can. Start with one area at a time and make incremental changes. No one is asking you to start training for a marathon (unless you want to). Changes don't have to be drastic to be meaningful and make a difference. Think about committing to a weekly game night with family. Or a no-screen Saturday. If that's too much, try a no-screen morning. Or try a one-mile walk with the dog before work each day. Or once a week, plan breakfast out with one of your kids. These are the kinds of changes my clients make, and I watch them grow happier. Any of these small tweaks can add so much to your well-being.

Don't believe me? Pick any one of the activities listed above or one of your choice. Close your eyes and imagine yourself following through with it. Are you smiling? My guess is you feel better just thinking about doing it. Imagine the difference you'll make in your well-being when you integrate such a change into your life.

Tending to your well-being is an ongoing project. As your life and career change, what you need to maintain well-being will change as well. So, stay on it.

If you need some extra motivation, consider joining the growing national movement in lawyer well-being. In December 2020, the Institute for Well-Being in Law (IWIL) was formed to carry on the movement launched by the national task force and the ABA. State and local bar associations are getting involved. Law firms have, and continue to sign onto the ABA's well-being pledge and committing to support the health and well-being of lawyers. The moment is here.

We can make well-being the standard for our profession, starting with ourselves.

HOLD YOURSELF ACCOUNTABLE

As hard as it is to convince lawyers that their career depends on their well-being, that's how easy it is for them to let their hard-won new habits of well-being slide. Because our culture doesn't place big value in this area yet—though that's changing—your taking care of yourself can feel self-indulgent. It is not. Don't leave maintaining your well-being up to chance. It's too important.

One of my clients, a self-professed workaholic, couldn't imagine putting effort into anything outside of work. Then she encountered health problems as she entered middle age. Even with the threat of declining health as a motivator, she loved working so much, she found it impossible to turn her work drive off and give herself over to recreation.

She solved her problem by coming up with the idea to make taking care of herself part of her job. With the same commitment she brought to her legal work each day, she decided to reconnect with her childhood love of basketball. She began with attending sporting events. She later branched out to explore other past loves, such as museums, theater, and music.

She held herself accountable by setting up a Pinterest page to chronicle her hard work having fun. Each week, she posted a picture just for herself. There she was at Longwood Gardens in Pennsylvania, the symphony, and a Philadelphia 76ers game. Within a year or so, she found she was getting good at relaxing. Her health improved. Her attitude—which she hadn't realized needed adjusting—improved. Her social connections grew, adding to her new sense of well-being and belonging. This led to lovely memories and documentary evidence that she doesn't spend her life working. Plus, her health, the original impetus, improved as well.

Until self-care becomes a habit, you, too, need to find ways to hold yourself accountable. You could make a pact with colleagues on the same path to improve their well-being to keep each other honest. Or make accountability for your well-being part of your work with your business coach or mentor. Or make a promise to model well-being practices for someone you mentor or a person in your life you couldn't bear to disappoint. Be sure anyone who is involved understands what you are doing, why you are doing it, and how important your well-being is to the career and life you want to have for yourself. This will help keep you true to your objectives.

Remember, it is not selfish to tend to your well-being. The exact opposite is true. You have a duty to your clients and the profession to be competent. Competence requires self-care. Just as no one wants a doctor who's been on duty for twenty-four hours making life-and-death decisions about them, no one wants a burned-out lawyer giving them consequential advice.

You are your career's best asset, and you need to treat yourself as such. Self-care is a marker that you have truly stepped out of default mode and into design mode. It's foundational to having a career and life that's yours.

LAW 10 IN BRIEF

- You can't be on top of your game when you are physically and mentally exhausted. Well-being is the underpinning of success in our lives and in our careers.
- The National Task Force on Lawyer Well-Being and the ABA recognize well-being as part of a lawyer's "ethical duty of competence" to clients. You have to be well to practice well.
- It's up to you to look after your well-being, which means prioritizing your health and yourself.
- The key to tending to your well-being is not time management, but self-management.

- Having what's important to you is by far more valuable than "having it all." So, it's imperative to your well-being that you know what's important to you.
- Your path to well-being begins with mining your assessments from Law 1 for data. And then using that data to evaluate your well-being in the six areas identified by the ABA.
- Once you see what you need to do, put a plan in place to do it.
- When it comes to well-being, incremental changes to your behavior are all that's needed to create big transformations. This is what makes Fitbit so popular. Little steps lead to big achievements.
- Hold yourself accountable for your well-being.
- Remember, you are your career's best asset, and you need to treat yourself as such.

In Conclusion: Overturning Precedent

Before employing the strategies in this book, my life in the law was a lot like the first line of Charles Dickens's novel *A Tale of Two Cities*: "It was the best of times, it was the worst of times . . ." At its best, for me, practicing law was an exciting intellectual challenge, an opportunity to help and make a difference, and to be in a profession filled with incredible, caring, and wickedly smart people. At its worst, practicing law was a daily drudgery from which there was no escape, free time, and no better times ahead that I could see, let alone count on.

That love-hate relationship so many lawyers have with their careers exists because—as this book has pointed out time and time again—the legal profession is filled with unwritten laws that trip us up or block us as we try to carve out a career and life for ourselves. Laws whose origins and purpose are lost to history. Laws that are never brought up, never discussed, and so we don't even know we need to navigate them. Such as, "Why is the norm to be overworked? Why isn't the track to partnership explained when we join the firm? Or when we interview? Why is it not drilled into our heads that the law is a business and requires entrepreneurial skills to advance and succeed, no matter the area of law you are in?"

I could go on, but it shouldn't really come as a shock to any of us that a profession built on reverence toward precedent would allow its workings and culture to be defined by "the way it's always been done."

In some ways, this is not a bad thing. We wouldn't want the law or our practice of it to bend to the latest fashion. In many ways, the rules that govern law schools and law practices are relics of the twentieth century—upholding a way of life that no longer exists. Many are impracticable, constrain potential and frustrate true talent, add unnecessary stress and pressure, and negate well-being. I would argue that these outmoded constructs limit the profession overall.

YOU RULE

All that said, the "way it's done" in the legal profession didn't change during my tenure to meet my needs and make my dreams come true. We can probably surmise it is not going to change that dramatically for you either. Fortunately for you, the set of ten laws in this book expose and make corrections for many of these "unwritten laws" (at least the ones concerned with career building). Taken together, the laws you find in these pages give you a detailed framework to put your career on the trajectory of your choosing. Let's review the laws.

Law 1: Assess the Situation
Determine where you are, why you are there, and if you want to stay there.

Law 2: Investigate Before You Commit
Making decisions based on nothing is how you got where you are—where you don't want to be in the first place. Collect data and use it in making your decisions from now on.

Law 3: Don't Double Down on Past Decisions
No matter how much you've put into it, if it isn't working for you, get rid of it.

Law 4: Curate Your Career

Doing a good job at your day job isn't enough to secure a career. You must invest time and effort in your professional development and growth as well. And if you get the chance, meet the governor. Don't let opportunities pass you by.

Law 5: Mind Your Mindset

Make your mind work for you, not against you. Be your own best advocate, not your own worst enemy.

Law 6: Hone Your Soft Skills

Getting along with others is crucial to your career. So, develop the necessary skills.

Law 7: Make It Rain

Creating revenue or influence in your organization gives you leverage. And leverage gives you options.

Law 8: It's Not Too Late

That is just an excuse. 'nuff said.

Law 9: Create an Environment for Change

Your environment can supercharge your growth—so make sure it does.

Law 10: Tend to Your Well-Being

Well-being is key to longevity, creativity, and enjoyment in your career and life. Cultivate it.

When it comes to your legal career—with these ten laws in your service—you now rule. With their guidance, you can escape the legal profession's precedents and build a career of your own design based on your own standards. In these laws, you find the strategies to stop defaulting to "the way things are done," to start questioning dictates that don't serve you, and to gather the information and new skills you need (skills also not taught in law school or on the job) to realize your vision for your career.

NO REGRETS. ONLY NECESSARY PASSAGES.

When you first opened this book, perhaps you were cursing the day you went to law school or your choice to enter the area of law you did—thinking you made a big mistake because you are not where you thought you'd be in life or in your professional career by now. I get that. When I was miserable in my job choice, I cursed the day I decided to go to law school, too, blaming the institution for all my unhappiness and problems.

But by now you understand regrets do not serve us, and they certainly don't serve our careers. They are a self-made path toward more of the thing we regret. Regret keeps your focus on the rearview mirror, on a past that never can be, and not the very real possibilities for your future. This is not to say to ignore the past. Far from it. But with the ten laws to guide you, you can use the past to build a future that fits—one you won't regret.

As I moved out of default mode and took charge of my own career, I found each step I'd taken—even the painful ones—were necessary passages. They provided me valuable data I needed to make the right choices for me moving forward. I found that I was grateful for each step (and misstep) of my journey. Every job I held, every boss I had (both disliked and loved) fed my evolution as a lawyer, as a coach, and as a human being.

For instance, when I really looked at it, my days in personal injury practice (the work I disliked the most in my career) weren't all bad. In some cases, on some days, the work was hugely gratifying—fighting for the underdog, getting justice, and paving a way for someone to survive. I must admit I did love aspects of it. Those aspects let me know I had a drive to help others. The litigation practice in general, however, proved unsuitably stressful, and most days the only meaning I found was like a speck of mica in a rock—occasional glitter, but still 90 percent rock. Both of these discoveries about myself greatly informed my decision to move into government law.

Practicing law in school districts and the Commonwealth of Pennsylvania, I got to see how government really works and its relationship with politics firsthand. Observing other government lawyers, lobbyists, and lawmakers, as well as chiefs of staff, opened my eyes to the many varied opportunities in law and the incredible places a JD can take a person in government.

Conducting workplace investigations in the corporate compliance department at Nemours Children's Health in Wilmington, Delaware, which I didn't love, taught me how to have extremely difficult professional conversations. I also learned the critical skill of listening as if life were at stake because, in the hospital setting where I worked, it was. These skills not only made me a better lawyer, but they also helped prepare me for a successful transition into coaching lawyers.

Once I came to accept the fact that I'd be the person making decisions about my career, I used information (data) from every job I'd ever held to discern preferences, expose my dislikes, take note of what I truly enjoyed doing and where I excelled. Instead of regretting my choices and berating myself for my past, I used my past as a guide to move myself forward to somewhere I wanted to be.

To regret law school and "the worst of times" in my career would be to regret the very things that opened so many doors—once I knew to knock on them—to a wholly fulfilling career and life in law, and now as a coach.

As a coach, my law school education and experience allowed me to understand my clients' world in a way nothing else could have, which helps them feel understood. I haven't just seen television shows about fictional lawyers. I've stood before judges, juries, and justices, too. I've experienced the pounding heart and sweaty palms at the utterance of two words by a judge, "Ms. Lefkowitz?" Though I don't practice anymore, I will always be a lawyer. It is how I think, the lens through which I see the world, a big part of who I am.

So, let's dump the regrets. They don't serve me and they don't serve you. Instead, treasure your past for the gold mine that it is. From this day forward, use your lived experience to inform decisions you make as you step up to preside over your career and set new precedents for yourself.

YOUR CAREER IS IN YOUR COURT NOW

In this book, you've seen how success looks different to everyone. From Kristen (Law 3), who had a passion for nonprofit law, to Charlie (Law 5), who transformed his idea of appellate advocacy into a firm worth over a million dollars and retired early to be with his family, to Sarah (Law 8), a paralegal who wanted to be a early education teacher. You can see the different roles that money, time, and personal interest played in these clients' lives and so in their decisions. How they leaned into their values and strengths to help them manifest the careers that were right for them and where they'd be successful. And why it is imperative that as you now take charge of your career, you, too, clearly define and know your feelings about money, time, and what interests you, as well as what you value and where your strengths lie.

Don't allow precedents or cultural norms or your own mindset prevent you from having the career you envision for yourself. When the powers that be—whether professors, partners, or the parrot in your own head—tell you things like, "You don't have free time," or "Working weekends is part of the job," or "You're not responsible for making it rain," question it. Question everything. Is this what you signed up for? Does what you are being asked to do serve your career vision? Is this what you want to be doing today? Next week? Ten years from now? If not, what are you going to do about it? In the end, your answers are the only ones that count.

Understand unequivocally that you don't have to give up the people and activities you love to make a living in the law—unless you want to. It is possible to practice law in a meaningful, satisfying way, without the law being your master, because you are your own master. Whenever you find you don't like the path you're on, even if it's one you have chosen for yourself, you can change it. Transformation is always available to you. You get to decide.

Note that you do not have to do all this alone. I didn't. Recognizing when you need help and asking for it are part of your professional growth, so don't be a "help-resistant" lawyer. When you open your eyes to it, you will see that help is everywhere. Seek out the mentors, allies, and coaches—whoever you need, whenever you need them.

You and your career are never done evolving. If you allow them to, these ten laws will continue to work for you and support you through every stage of your career. Use them. They have moved me and hundreds of my clients from careers by default into careers and lives by design.

Your career is in your court now. If you want things to be different than they are, you have it within your power to start laying down the law, overturning precedents that don't serve your vision, and setting new ones that do. You have it within your power to stop defaulting and start designing a law career and a life destined to deliver the best of times.

P.S. I wouldn't be a coach if I didn't want to hear from you. If you wish, you can reach out to me at Dena@AchievementByDesign.com. I'd love to hear about how you've put these laws into action and how your career by design is progressing.

Acknowledgments

To Murray and Sylvia Lefkowitz, for keeping an open dictionary in our living room and repeatedly sending me to it, creating a lifelong love affair with words and reading.

To the teachers of the School District of Philadelphia and librarians of the Free Library of Philadelphia, particularly the Wynnefield Library, my home away from home growing up.

To my clients, who are the real teachers in this book.

To Beth Brand, book coach and editor extraordinaire. Thank you for expertly (and gently) guiding me to the finish line and getting me through those "glazed doughnut" moments. This book would not exist without you.

To Clare Day, for being my dear friend, anchor, and supporting my coaching business while I wrote this book.

To Jasper, who walked with me while I practiced for the Pennsylvania Supreme Court, sat by my side while I wrote this book, and gave me unconditional love and joy.

To Michael Lefkowitz, Jay Lefkowitz, Ruth Lefkowitz, Caroline Semancik, J. Murray Elwood, Pat Talese, Jackie B. Sparkman, Esq., former mayor of Philadelphia Michael A. Nutter, Diane Castelbuono, Kimberly A. Caputo, Esq., Barry Fox, Terry L. Mutchler, Esq., Sheila Kutner, Marjorie Johnson, Suzanne Perry, Jamie Sussel

Turner, Joel Roberts, Heidi Roberts and the Gravitas Group, Barbra DiJohn, Linda Anderson, Esq., Steve Sparks, Esq., Terri Hoopes, and James J. Rohn, Esq.: You made an indelible mark on my life and I am grateful.

About the Author

Dena Lefkowitz, Esq., PCC, is the founder of Achievement by Design, LLC, a leading coaching firm focused on helping lawyers find career direction and partnering with law firms to help their attorneys develop into rainmakers. She has been featured in *Forbes* magazine and the *Huffington Post*, and regularly contributed to Law.com for seven years. The former lawyer of twenty-five years reinvented herself from being a civil litigator to general counsel for state government. Dena then transitioned from being a lawyer to helping other lawyers. She was awarded her juris doctor from Temple University School of Law, graduated from the College of Executive Training, and earned certification from Harvard University Kennedy School of Government in Executive Education and Leadership. Dena lives in Media, Pennsylvania, and can be reached at https://achievementbydesign.com.